f

father's financial favour

by

T. W. Appel

father's financial favour
Copyright 2004 by T. W. Appel
ISBN# 1-59352-109-X

Contact author at:
Terry Appel
c/o Harvest Crusade International
P.O. Box 639
Mona Vale
Sydney NSW 2103
Australia

Creative and Publishing Services by:
Christian Services Network
1975 Janich Ranch Court
El Cajon, CA 92019
(toll free) 1-866-484-6184
(website) CSNbooks.com

The spelling of "favour" and "honour" in the titles is faithful to the Bible. However, in the text the American English spelling is used whenever the words are not in quotation marks.

Unless otherwise identified, all Scripture quotations are from the New King James Version of the Holy Bible.

cover design and
photography by

design

www.leannehunt.com

dedication

I would like to dedicate this book to my wife Faye and my children Jonathan, Sarah and Bethany who have put up with a lot from me over the last couple of years as I have been totally focused in getting this book to its final conclusion.

contents

ACKNOWLEDGMENTS vii
FOREWORD ix
INTRODUCTION xi
   from orphan to sonship

CHAPTER ONE 19
   the father's house

CHAPTER TWO 43
   the father's finances

CHAPTER THREE 61
   the father's honour

CHAPTER FOUR 77
   the father's expectation

CHAPTER FIVE 107
   the father's favour

CHAPTER SIX 131
   the father's delight

REFERENCES 157

acknowledgments

Special appreciation to Tamsin Haes who has worked tirelessly and sacrificed so much of her personal time on the material of this book. Her dedication and her enthusiasm has been inspiring. Thank you for making me look so good. Also a special thanks to her husband David for his kindness and patience through the editing of the book.

foreword

I consider it a great privilege to endorse Terry Appel's new book *father's financial favour – from poverty to generosity*.

After having been exposed to many teaching ministries around the globe which focus on biblically based insights regarding finances, I can wholeheartedly say Terry's book is a real breakthrough for two important reasons.

First, the insights Terry relates concerning God's ways of stewarding finances and resources are life changing and fresh. While many merely restate others' teachings, Terry's insights are genuinely profound in helping us understand both exactly what God stated, and what the implications were in the time of the Bible's cultures.

Not only with our ministry, but with our family finances as well, Terry's teachings have helped bring about substantial breakthroughs.

Equally important, however, all of Terry's teaching and ministry comes under the umbrella of a great focus on the Father Heart of God. While many teachings on finances have been true in the points, they have led the recipient off track due to a primary focus on money, wealth, and outward success.

Terry's ministry, in contrast, just as the title states, is characterized by 2 Corinthians 9:8 that the sower may have an abundance for every good work! Terry's goals for those he ministers to is not the wealth of the world, but rather the wealth of the Kingdom – that we may be givers, like our Father in Heaven. And along the way we discover it really is more blessed to give than it is to receive.

I believe this book is a must read for all who desire to be both good stewards of God's provision and know the wonderful provision of Father God for their lives.

Marc A. Dupont
Mantle of Praise Ministries, Inc.
Dayton, Ohio
June 20, 2004

Introduction

from orphan to sonship

This book, *father's financial favour* is about how God took an orphan from poverty to generosity, made him a son, and through this son, released some of His wisdom about how to manage finances in the Father's house. My heart's desire is that it would bless you and help you to come to know, and to walk in, financial freedom.

First, I would like to personally acknowledge a few men of God who have had a very big influence on my life. The person with the most influence was my Senior Pastor Frank Houston, during his time as senior minister of Christian Life Centre in Sydney.

In January of 1980 I surrendered my life to Jesus Christ and started on a road and a life that I would recommend to anyone. From the very first day of my commitment to Christ, I felt that all I had ever done and all that I had ever been involved in was totally removed from my heart. It was as if someone had reached deep down inside my heart and surgically cut away the stain from my past and then filled me with an assurance of my future – and at the same time flooding me with a peace that passed all understanding.

I didn't know how to articulate it at the time, but I realize now that from that point, all things had become new about my life. I know that *"if anyone is in Christ, he is a new creation; old things have passed away; behold, all things have become new"* (2 Corinthians 5:17).

It was not long before I was on the path of the ministry that the Lord had reserved for me. Under the guiding hand of Pastor Frank Houston, and by his life's example, God's calling on my life was beginning to take shape.

Pastor Frank modeled a lifestyle of giving which impacted me in such a way that I adopted many of the truths that he lived for my own life. Having been brought up as an orphan I had no role model to shape my life and future, and so it is with thanks that I acknowledge Pastor Frank Houston, and honor him.

In 1994 I met another man of God who had a great bearing on my life and ministry. That man was John Arnott, the senior Pastor of Toronto Airport Christian Fellowship. During my many years in the ministry I have shared what Jesus has done for me and how the Holy Spirit has used me in different areas of the gifts of the spirit. Despite this, I knew that there was a lack in my life. For years I carried around in me a deep yearning for more, but didn't understand what this "more" was.

I would often be in a worship service, reaching out with all my heart loving and worshipping Jesus, however I could feel an unseen ceiling over my head. It felt like this barrier was stopping me from breaking through into an intimacy that was mine by birthright.

It was not until God led me to meet John and Carol Arnott that I discovered the answer. In the month of November 1994 on the floor of a church at the end of a runway in Toronto, Canada, I met God in a way that impacted me and introduced Father's love for me. I had come all the way from Sydney in Australia because I was hungry for more of God and had heard that God was doing something in that church.

On the floor that night the Father came and overshadowed me like a wave, which rolled in for hours. He took me back to when I was about eighteen months old, and the memory was as clear to me as the day that it happened. At this time my mother had abandoned me, and left me in an orphanage.

One day there was a storm, and in the eyes of a little child with all the lightning and thunder it looked like the end of the world had come. I did not know what to do, where to turn, or where to go, so I hid under a railway carriage to escape the storm. It was at this moment that the incredible gift of innocence that God gives to all of us was stolen from my life.

Deserted and alone, I was so devastated there were no arms to hold me, no chest to lay my head on, and no one to prevent this gift from being stolen. As a little child, I felt my emotions being raped and the pain penetrated my very being. From that day forward, the pain never left me. Every night I would grind my teeth and rock myself to sleep to try and find some comfort.

That fateful night at Toronto on the floor of the church, God began a healing work in me that continues to this day. He showed me why the ceiling seemed to be over my head during times of worship.

What had happened was, that when Satan, the thief, stole my innocence, I had also lost the ability to be intimate with God. Without true intimacy there is no fulfillment in worship. I was like Tamar of the Bible (2 Samuel 13:20b) who was desolate and barren in intimacy. I had a brief understanding of how Eve must have felt when the thief stole her innocence in the Garden of Eden, and she consequently lost the intimacy she had with God.

On that floor I cried and cried, and cried some more. These were not just tears of sadness, or even loss, but a river of pain that had attached itself to my soul. Deep within me, the pain began to seep out of my heart. My overwhelming feelings of rejection and of being deserted left me. The holes in my emotions began to heal. As in a vision, I saw myself again as a little child and I saw myself at the feet of this huge man who was sitting down. I began to climb up his legs and into his lap. As I did this, I felt for the first time in my life, what it was to feel the arms of a man around me. I'm not able to put into words the warmth that flooded my soul. It swamped me and flowed over me again and again, like waves of the sea. I felt cocooned, safe and protected. I felt whole.

At that moment I felt the urge to look up and see whose lap I had climbed into. To my amazement the lap was my own! At that split second I gazed up, a joy enveloped me. There was a realization in my soul that for the first time in my life I accepted myself just the way I was.

Now a new word has been added to my Christian vocabulary and that word is "Father". In the time that I spent with John and Carol Arnott, they brought me to a place in God that returned my innocence, and with that, my intimacy with God the Father was restored. There is now no ceiling over me and by His grace I walk in intimacy with Him as His son. I want to extend a special thanks to Carol for all the ministry time she put in for me.

The other man of God who has had a great bearing on my life is Rodney Howard Brown. His contagious attitudes to God and to the resources of the kingdom, his openness, and his humility have challenged my life.

Rodney carries a prophetic message for this generation, particularly in the realm of kingdom finances. His attitude to finances challenged me to have a fresh look at the way the finances of the Father's house are to be managed. I personally received his messages on finances as a prophetic word to the Church.

As a result, it has brought great blessing to my life, to my family and to the church that God has given me the privilege to pastor. Jesus said that:

He who receives a prophet in the name of a prophet shall receive a prophet's reward. And he who receives a righteous man in the name of a righteous man shall receive a righteous man's reward.

(Matthew 10:41)

And so it is with a grateful heart to God that I thank these people who have so influenced my life and ministry.

Chapter 1

the father's house

For God so loved the world that He gave His only begotten son, that whoever believes in Him should not perish but have everlasting life.

(John 3:16)

I believe this Scripture is the foundation for this great subject of freedom for our lives (whether in finances or any other area). One of the great attributes of God is giving, and He paid the total cost to bring about a total release in every area of our lives. As such, He has set the pattern for us, as His children, to follow.

The purpose of this book is to explore this concept of financial freedom and to demonstrate that anyone can walk in the reality of financial freedom, no matter what socioeconomic situation they find themselves in.

In the Father's house all His sons are equal, and all share in His inheritance. In the parable of the prodigal son the Father said *"Son, you are always with me, and all that I have is yours"* (Luke 15:31). However, the sad reality is many don't seem to walk in this blessing that the Father has for them.

There are many and varied reasons for this. In some cases it results from ignorance through wrong teaching. In other cases it's because the Father's sons do not know who they are, or what they have in the house, as *"many as received Him, to them gave He the right to become the children of God, even to those that believe on His name"* (John 1:12). I love the way the King James Version of the Bible uses the word "sons" instead of "children".

Please note that throughout this book whenever I use the title "sons" I am using it in a non-gender specific way. For while the Bible states it is the "sons" that inherit, remember that *"there is neither Jew nor Greek, there is neither slave nor free, there is neither male nor female; for you are all one in Christ Jesus"* (Galatians 3:28).

In order to bring about changes to our financial dilemmas, there must be a change in how we respond to what the Father has laid out for us in His house. It has to be the Father's way or no way, for He is committed to our financial freedom.

When the subject of money is broached, people respond in many different ways, and these responses often reveal what is in peoples' hearts. In the Father's house, for instance, tithing is a natural part of an ongoing relationship with Him, as His sons return to Him what is His. Yet so many stumble at this first step, arguing their point of view either from the letter of the law or from the position of grace.

There is, of course, a little truth in each of these viewpoints. The first group keeps to the letter of the law, that is, they tithe on every financial transaction. However they have no understanding of what the tithe does or does not do for them relationally.

The second group makes the law for themselves. In other words, they decide what they will do with the financial resources that Father has given – they decide where, when and if they will give. This group is losing sight of one very important fact – that what they have is not theirs in the first place, because *"The silver is Mine, and the gold is Mine," says the Lord of Hosts* (Haggai 2:8). Therefore in the harshest sense I would have to conclude that both of these views can be so wrong, and neither will bring a person into the financial freedom they seek.

Let me say right from the outset that financial freedom in the Father's house is not about formulas. On the contrary, it is about taking hold of the patterns that God has set out for us in His Word. Historically, the Church has focused on the development of formulas to try and get from God what He has promised, rather than focusing on developing maturity and living according to the patterns that He has already set out for us.

Formulas are only good for children who can't digest solid food:

> *For though by this time you ought to be teachers, you need someone to teach you again the first principles of the oracles of God; and you have come to need milk and not solid food. For everyone who partakes only of milk is unskilled in the word of righteousness, for he is a babe.*
> (Hebrews 5:12:13)

As newborn babes, *"desire the pure milk of the word, that you may grow thereby"* (1 Peter 2:2). In focusing on formulas, we have raised a generation of children in the Church who have not matured into sons in the Father's house.

While we remain as children, there is no

realization of the inheritance that is ours, for the heir, *"as long as he is a child, does not differ at all from a slave, though he is master of all"* (Galatians 4:1). If we want to live in the freedom that is already ours, then we must live according to the patterns and principles set out for us in His Word, rather than seeking out formulas. For instance, there are so many books written about how to hear the voice of God. However, as good as these books may be, the simple answer set out for us in the Bible is to listen!

We are His, and all things are His. If we keep that in mind, we will always be aware of how incredibly blessed we are. All things *"were made by Him; and without Him was not any thing made that was made"* (John 1:3). For *"of Him, and through Him, and to Him, are all things: to whom be glory forever"* (Romans 11:36). For by Him *"were all things created, that are in heaven, and that are in earth, visible and invisible, whether they be thrones, or dominions, or principalities, or powers: all things were created by Him, and for Him"* (Colossians 1:16).

If we understand that all things belong to God, we come to realize that God is not interested in dollars and cents as such. Rather, He is very interested in the heart, and our attitudes. He who inhabits the heavens is not made one dollar richer by what we give to Him for the extension of His kingdom, and what He has worked into our hearts has no monetary value. Let me pose this question. when it comes to giving, what is the most important thing to you? Is it the amount you give, or is it your heart attitude?

In the gospel of Mark, chapter twelve, Jesus relays an account of two different types of givers. One giver put in a great amount, the other put in just two mites. I wonder if the person that impressed Jesus the most would be the same person that would have impressed us?

Jesus called His disciples to Himself and said to them:

> *...assuredly, I say to you that this poor widow has put in more than all those who have given to the treasury; for they all put in out of their abundance, but she out of her poverty put in all that she had, her whole livelihood.*
>
> (Mark 12:43-44)

The widow put in, despite her position of need, and this heart attitude impressed Jesus. She gave from a position of sacrifice, not from a position of abundance. Her giving was centered not in the amount but in the heart. What an incredible thing to think that the Lord showed up just to watch the giving of a widow.

In the Father's house it is always the heart that impresses Him, not the amount. This widow had learned one of the greatest truths of the Father's house – trust. So the first truth that we need to adopt for our lives in order to be free financially is that the Father is after our heart attitude, and the second is that we can trust the Father.

Just let me say this before we move on. One of the great things that the Father wants to do in our lives is to get us to a place where we will trust Him. Please don't be frightened of this word. "Trust" does not mean that the Father is coming to take everything from you, or that He wants you to be poor.

The trust He is trying to impart to us is a trust that brings contentment to our lives. I love how the psalmist David put it when he stated *"the Lord is my shepherd; I shall not want"* (Psalm 3:1).

The Apostle Paul put it this way:

> *...not that I speak in regard to need, for I have learned in whatever state I am, to be content: I know how to be abased, and I know how to abound, everywhere and in all things I have learned both to be full and to be hungry, both to abound and to suffer need.*
>
> (Philippians 4:11-12)

father's financial favour

In the Father's house He is developing His sons to be content when they abound, and content when they go through times of being abased. It is not a matter of how much we have, or do not have; it is about being content in the state in which we find ourselves. This is the trust the Father is looking for, and *"godliness with contentment is great gain"* (1 Timothy 6:6).

I now want to take you back to a time in the Bible from the Old Testament, but first a word about the relationship between the Old and New Testaments. I am sad to say I have met some Christians through the years who believe that because the old covenant is replaced by the new, they think they have the liberty to throw away the Old Testament, and their confession is that they don't need it any more. However, these well meaning believers have lost sight of the very reason for the Bible.

It is explained wonderfully for us in 2 Timothy 3:16 that:

> *...all scripture is given by inspiration of God, and is profitable for doctrine, for reproof, for correction, for instruction in righteousness.*

Notice if you will, that it says "all scripture". Jesus said *"think not that I am come to destroy the law, or the prophets: I am not come to destroy, but to*

the father's house

fulfill" (Matthew 5:17). So don't throw the old away, for in the Old Testament the new is concealed.

As we know, the old covenant was made with Moses and with Israel. But there was a time before this covenant, where man was moved by his conscience. This period is known as "The Age of Conscience," and it is at this time in man's history with God that I want to start addressing this subject.

The book of Genesis (chapter 1) describes how God made man. This was the beginning of God's relationship with man, but things went wrong. Adam sinned, and as a result, all men (as we are descendants of Adam) rebelled against God. God then sent the flood, out of which only eight were saved. This represented another beginning for the earth. Out of this remnant came the construction of the tower of Babel, yet another act of rebellion against God, and as a result the Lord scattered people over all the earth with different tongues or languages.

So what was God doing between the time of Adam and His covenant with Moses? This was the time in which Abraham lived. At this time, God did not have arrangements with any particular nation, or group of people. However, He did have certain arrangements with individuals, and one of these individuals was Abraham.

father's financial favour

Abraham was to be the new starting point. He was to be the father of a people who would trust and rely on God's abundance and God's goodness. A people who would be full of faith and be well pleasing to Him, because:

> *...without faith it is impossible to please Him, for he who comes to God must believe that He is, and that He is a rewarder of those who diligently seek Him.*
>
> (Hebrews 11:6)

Interestingly, Scripture shows that many things started with Abraham, including the subject of tithing, (which we will cover in another chapter), so it is important to see where Abraham fits into the scheme of things. In God's economy, Abraham represented a new beginning.

God spoke to Abraham and said:

> *Get out of your country, from your family, and from your father's house, to a land that I will show you.*
>
> (Genesis 12:1)

The writer of Hebrews tells us that:

> *...by faith Abraham obeyed when he was called to go out to the place which he would receive as an inheritance. He went out, not knowing where he was going.*
>
> (Hebrews 11:8)

the father's house

Why Abraham obeyed, the Bible does not tell us, but there would be no doubt that he would have heard the infallible nature of God's voice.

This was not a small thing that God asked Abraham to do. He was instructed by God at the age of seventy five years to get up and start all over again. Also, the Bible does not imply that before this encounter Abraham even knew God. But it does say that he responded and abandoned himself to God and His purposes.

Abraham obeyed without knowing. Obedience is the true test of a man's heart. Will we, despite our circumstances, obey the word of the Lord, especially when it comes to the subject of money? Obedience is not so difficult when we are doing well or when our lives are stable financially. Often the real test comes when we are going through lean times in our lives and the challenge that confronts us is whether we will remain faithful to what the Lord says. It is in the crucible of obedience that our hearts are molded and shaped. Whether we feel like it or not, God wants us to listen and to obey.

Abraham just got up and obeyed without knowing where he was going. This is a major key for us to take hold of. From this first act of obedience, this first act of faith, God opened up to Abraham a

father's financial favour

life of victorious living. He opened up to Abraham great desires, dreams and ambitions. God also gave to him the great commission so that he could bring forth the plans of God for his generation. Through Abraham and his seed would all the nations be blessed.

All the promises of God were in Abraham's son, Isaac. Yet such was the heart of Abraham in obedience towards God that:

> *...by faith Abraham, when he was tested, offered up Isaac, and he who had received the promises offered up his only begotten son.*
>
> (Hebrews 11:17)

Abraham's life is a great challenge to all who claim or name the Lord as their own. After walking with the Lord all the years that we have, the test of our love for Him will always come down to this one question. Will we give up all that He has given to us? In other words, are we willing to turn our backs on all that He has promised us, because He asks us to?

If God asked us "What will you do for Me, knowing that all the gold and silver is Mine, will you obey Me despite your circumstances? Will you give to Me unashamedly that which I ask for?" How would we respond, keeping in mind that at the heart of all that God does is giving?

The strength of Abraham's life was that he had an anchor in his heart. That anchor was assurance, and Abraham's assurance was based upon the faithfulness of God. Despite what he faced, Abraham knew that God was faithful. Abraham was assured that even if his son died, he knew that God could raise him from the dead to fulfill his plans and purposes.

Abraham said to his young men:

Stay here with the donkey; the lad and I will go yonder and worship, and we will come back to you.
(Genesis 22:5)

He makes this statement despite knowing that God had asked him to sacrifice his son on Mount Moriah. Such was the anchor of his soul that he was not persuaded to disobey God, despite God's seemingly horrendous request.

This was the new beginning that God wanted. Out of the loins of Abraham would come a people who would abandon themselves to God, to His plans and to His vision. A company of people who would not be tied to land, or governed by anything that the world had to offer, not even its wealth. This was a people who would not allow their own dreams to hinder the purposes of God for their lives. People who would forsake all things to live a life in which they would trust God, and only God.

Now before we look at this further, let me ask you to take the time to ponder and come to an understanding of this next point. Because we are discussing finances, and because the word "abandon" has been used, there is no suggestion here that you should let go of your life to such an extent that you have to live in poverty. Poverty is never the purpose or the call of God for His children. Poverty is a curse.

The word teaches us that we can trust God. The Book of Philippians states:

> *My God shall supply all your need according to his riches in glory by Christ Jesus.*
>
> (Philippians 4:19)

Jesus told us to pray *"Father give us this day our daily bread"* (Matthew 6:11). So we see that God makes provision for us and does not expect us to live in poverty.

Abraham was a very rich man when he was being put through this test of the heart. The test was not so much about what he had, but who he was. Was he a man given over to the plans of God? Did he have a lifestyle of giving? Did he have God's agenda? His heart is exposed for us as we see that it was:

> ...*by faith he dwelt in the land of promise as in a foreign country, dwelling in tents with Isaac and Jacob, the heirs with him of the same promise.*
> (Hebrews 11:9)

We can see that Abraham's heart was focused on the giver of the land, rather than the land itself. He lived in the light of eternity, and he:

> ...*waited for the city which has foundations, whose builder and maker is God.*
> (Hebrews 11:10)

As the people of God, you and I should do no less. If we are to expect great things in eternity, then our focus should be on eternal things.

When we look at the life and times of Abraham, we can mistakenly think he had it fairly easy, but he had his problems. One of these was Lot, his nephew. Lot was a real headache for his uncle, but at the same time, he was a catalyst that caused Abraham to rely more on God. Often God will use our problems or mistakes to bring hidden issues to the surface in our lives, so that we can deal with them.

father's financial favour

Let us take a moment to look at these two men described in Genesis (chapter thirteen, verses two and five). Abraham was "very rich in livestock, in silver, and in gold". Lot also "had flocks and herds and tents". Did you pick up the difference between these two men? They were both blessed with livestock (or provision).

However, only Abraham had the metals silver and gold which must be refined in fire. In other words, Abraham had the precious things – the things you have to dig for, the things that cost you something. Abraham moved and trusted in the things that were not seen, that is, he was a man of faith. Lot went out in the strength of Abraham's faith, and of course the blessing of God fell on Lot because he was under Abraham's covering.

The Bible tells us that one day there was a skirmish between the herdsmen of the two men. Abraham in his loving and giving way said:

...let there not be any strife between me and thee for we are kinsmen.

(Genesis 13:8)

Abraham's heart was to let Lot make the choice of the land before them, even though it should have been his choice because of the call of God. Abraham would settle for what was left. This is the heart of a magnanimous man. A man or woman of God never has to justify themselves nor defend their position.

In response to Abraham's offer:

Lot lifted his eyes and saw all the plain of Jordan, that it was well watered everywhere (before the Lord destroyed Sodom and Gomorrah) like the garden of the Lord, like the land of Egypt as you go toward Zoar.

(Genesis 13:10)

Here the true heart of Lot was revealed. Notice that he followed what his eyes had beheld. He walked by sight. He lifted up his eyes. A man of faith does not walk by sight. Lot was a taker and was moved by what he saw.

Giving is not governed by what is seen. Hebrews 11:1 states that *"faith is the substance of things hoped for, the evidence of things not seen"*. True giving is a deep heart change that causes one to always be responding no matter what the circumstances. Lot's actions are in direct contrast to Abraham, the giver.

The heart of the giver reveals a life which never depends upon circumstances, as they have settled the matter and have decided that they will walk by faith and not by sight. At this stage Lot was not walking in the same freedom as his uncle, so he made his decision according to what pleased him and what was right in his own eyes. He made his decision to settle in the plains of Jordan.

Remember that Abraham was the one with the call of God on his life to leave his kindred and home. It was not his nephew Lot who was called. However, a surrendered heart does not need to exercise its rights. Giving must be a lifestyle, regardless of how circumstances appear.

If our giving only depends upon favorable circumstances in our lives, then we will be constantly harassed by what we see, and that which starts off as pleasing to the eye can often be our downfall. Just ask Adam's wife Eve! By dwelling on what pleased the eye she brought about the downfall of man.

> *So when the woman saw that the tree was good for food, that it was pleasant to the eyes, and a tree desirable to make one wise, she took of its fruit and ate. She also gave to her husband with her, and he ate.*
>
> (Genesis 3:6)

If that doesn't convince you, look at Lot's wife. In disobedience to the command of God, she turned back for just one more look at what she left behind and because of this was turned into a pillar of salt. Our focus has to be on what the Father wants so that faith arises, rather than the circumstances that often rob us of our ability to trust the Father and see His plan for our lives.

Both Eve and Lot's wife's eyes were filled with circumstances and they both missed what God had for them. Jesus said:

> *No one, having put his hand to the plough, and looking back, is fit for the kingdom of God.*
> (Luke 9:62)

Lot is a good picture of someone who thinks he is owed something in the Kingdom of God and then has the right to make demands. However, Jesus urges us to:

> *...seek first the kingdom of God and His righteousness, and all these things shall be added to you.*
> (Matthew 6:33)

I don't believe in demanding anything from God or in trying to twist His arm. The people chosen by God did that in the wilderness, despite the fact that God was providing for their every need. Their greed demanded more than what was being provided. They demanded that God give them meat, and He gave it to them, but with the getting they got leanness for their souls.

father's financial favour

This still happens today. When we put our jobs ahead of God, or make demands for things, all that we end up with is leanness for our souls, because our eyes are focused only on the temporal.

Lot could not see the corruption that was behind the walls of the cities nearby, and he did not discern the seduction of Sodom and Gomorrah. As you continue to read about him in Genesis, you will find that because his decisions were birthed in what he saw (rather than in faith) it cost him everything he had, even his family. Lot lost the lot! Those who were not lost in the city, or who didn't turn into a pillar of salt, ended up lost in a cave where burning incest took over their hearts (Genesis 19:30-38). What a high price Lot paid to walk by sight!

Let's look at God's response to the magnanimous way that Abraham treated Lot. How did God respond to his selfless act of giving? We see that the...

> *Lord said to Abraham, after Lot had separated from him, lift your eyes now and look from the place where you are; northward, southward, eastward, and westward; for all the land which you see I give to you and your descendants forever.*
>
> (Genesis 13:14-15)

In other words, even though Abraham had given away what was rightfully his, God honored his trust and giving heart by bestowing on him everything his eye could see.

Now let's revisit the fourteenth chapter of Genesis and see how Abraham's headache, Lot, is doing. We find him in the wrong spot at the wrong time. The kings Elam and Tidal had defeated the kings of Sodom and Gomorrah, then captured Lot and all his goods and carried them away. Upon hearing of this event, Abraham armed himself, took three hundred and eighteen of his servants and went to put the matter right. The Word records that Abraham won the battle, and he brought back the women and all the goods that were taken.

On Abraham's return from the battle a very interesting thing happened. Two kings came out to greet him. One king whose name was Melchizedek had attributes of peace and righteousness. The other king's name was Bera. He was the king of Sodom. He was a king of looseness, compromise and of death.

The king of peace brought wine and bread to Abraham, and they had a communion service to give honor and glory to the Lord. Abraham received a blessing from this king. In response to this wonderful time of fellowship, Abraham gave a tithe of all that he had to Melchizedek. This is the first time in the Bible that this word "tithe" is mentioned.

father's financial favour

The Hebrew meaning of the word tithe is "a tenth". We will cover this subject in some detail in the next chapter which deals with the Father's finances.

Abraham gave in response to the fellowship and the communion of the bread and the wine, which is a wonderful picture of a covenant. Abraham responded out of a heart that was used to giving. He spontaneously gave ten percent of all he had. He knew that the Lord is the possessor of heaven and earth, and he could have just as easily given nine tenths. However, it was not the percentage he gave that was the issue, but his attitude in giving and responding from a generous heart.

Just like Abraham, every time we are faced with a major decision about our lives, the spirit of these two kings will be there to influence our hearts. One offers covenant, the other offers this world's goods, but with a catch.

Notice what the king of Sodom offers to give, despite the fact that it was not his to give anymore as he was dispossessed of it. The king of Sodom said to Abram, *"Give me the persons'* **souls** *(bold added) and take the goods for yourself"* (Genesis 14:21). He was basically saying "You can have all the goods; just give me the souls of men. You can have what you want, just demand it, but don't touch the souls, they're mine."

Take note of Abraham's reply when he says:

I will take nothing, from a thread to a sandal strap, and I will not take anything that is yours, lest you should say, 'I have made Abram rich'.
(Genesis 14:23)

Please understand that the prince of this world is not wholly after the goods of this world either, he wants peoples' souls. Abraham wanted his blessing and riches where it counted, that is, with God.

The Father's house is a place of covenant, liberty and liberality. It is a place where our hearts are continually exposed for scanning and where resources are continually shared. The heart of our Father is a heart of giving, and we are to respond in kind with giving as He gives.

It is because of our relationship with Him that we know we can trust him with every facet of our lives. It is our integrity which will position us financially because we are walking in obedience to God.

father's financial favour

Chapter 2

the father's finances

In the previous chapter we established from Scripture that all the gold and the silver in the world already belong to God. Therefore, if we were to give Him all the money we have at our disposal it would not make Him one dollar richer. Those of us who have accepted Jesus as our Lord and Savior now live in the Father's house and therefore we operate in a different financial economy from the rest of the world.

Within God's economy there are incredible freedoms, but as with any economy there are some guidelines that need to be followed in order to reap its benefits. The guideline I want to focus on in this chapter is tithing.

There is a wonderful picture of this set out for us

in the third chapter of Malachi, and it demonstrates what our obedience opens up for us. We are to:

> Bring all the tithes into the storehouse, that there may be food in My house, and try Me now in this, says the Lord of hosts, if I will not open for you the windows of heaven and pour out for you such blessing that there will not be room enough to receive it. And I will rebuke the devourer for your sakes, so that he will not destroy the fruit of your ground, nor shall the vine fail to bear fruit for you in the field, says the Lord of hosts. And all nations will call you blessed, for you will be a delightful land says the Lord of hosts.
> (Malachi 3:10–12)

We will now look at each of the principles and benefits of this truth in more detail.

bringing tithes into the storehouse...

When we look at the Father's house and its financial structure, we discover that all through Scripture God requires that His sons return to Him a tithe of everything He has entrusted to them. The Hebrew word for tithe is "a tenth", so a "tithe" represents a tenth of all that God has given us.

Please note that throughout this chapter I use the

word "return" rather than "give". The reason behind it is simple – we cannot give to God that which already belongs to Him, but we can bring it and return it to Him. In other words, to return is to bring back that which belongs to another. For the same reason I never use the phrase "my tithe" because it implies ownership. It is always the Lord's tithe and never mine. Where we place the emphasis may be a warning to us to check the attitudes of our heart to see who really has ownership.

The tithe has first place and is always a tithe of everything that comes our way. In teaching this truth around the world I have been asked many times concerning the correct amount to tithe. For example, "Should I tithe before or after I have paid what the Government requires for tax?" I love to respond with Jesus' own words:

> ...render therefore unto Caesar the things which are Caesar's; and unto God the things that are God's.
> (Matthew 22:21)

The key here is that it is not so much that we have to give ten percent of all of our income (as we have seen, all the gold and silver is the Lord's anyway), but that we put Him first and give all that He requires of us.

There is an expectation that we keep proper financial records, responding as sons of God out of our relationship with Him. As we saw in the previous chapter, it was Abraham's response toward the Lord that was the important issue.

giving the father first place...

In the previous chapter, we established that the Father does not need our money, so it is not a matter of the Father wanting what we have, but a desire in His heart for us to relate to Him in a full, open and true relationship. What the return of the tithe does is to declare that we, His sons, have put the Father in first place. In other words, the tithe teaches us to put God first in our lives.

We discover the spirit of this principle of putting God first in the Garden of Eden, where:

> *The Lord God took the man and put him in the Garden of Eden to tend and keep it. And the Lord God commanded the man saying;*
>
> *Of every tree of the garden you may freely eat: but of the tree of the knowledge of good and evil you shall not eat, for in the day that you eat of it you shall surely die.*
>
> (Genesis 2:15-17)

Notice that God gave them all the trees in the garden, and they could enjoy the fruit of every tree except the tree of the knowledge of good and evil.

As a father, God gave all provision for His children, Adam and Eve, to enjoy in the garden so that they would be blessed and provided for. Then God said to Adam, *"The tree of the knowledge of good and evil you shall not eat"* (Genesis 2:17). God, according to His divine power, *"has given to us all things that pertain to life and godliness, through the knowledge of Him who called us by glory and virtue"* (2 Peter 1:3).

Here we have the first principle of growth and honor, that is, the requirement that the son respond in obedience to his Father. This tree that God pointed out to Adam was to be the teacher of obedience; it was to be the key to the blessing of God and the continued unhindered fellowship between Father and son.

Remember that the Father gave Adam and Eve all the trees to enjoy, including the tree of life, but the tree of the knowledge of good and evil was to remain the domain of God alone. So we can see that God trusted His son Adam to honor Him and put Him first. God trusted that His son would grow in nature and character to be more like Him through obedience to His request. The tree of the knowledge of good and evil was put there to remind God's children that He was to have first place.

Although the principle of first place can be found in the Garden of Eden, the first mention of the word "tithe" is used in conjunction with the patriarch Abraham, as we saw in the previous chapter.

> *Then Melchizedek king of Salem brought out bread and wine; he was the priest of God Most High. And he blessed him and said blessed be Abram of God Most High, possessor of heaven and earth; and blessed be God Most High, who has delivered your enemies into your hand and he gave him a tithe of all.*
>
> (Genesis 14:18-20)

Here we see that Abraham honored God and gave a tenth or a tithe of all that he had. He did this in response to the blessing of the wine and the bread (which represents covenant), and his desire to put God first.

As new covenant people, that is, as Christians, we also should respond to the bread and the wine because:

> *If you are Christ's seed, then you are Abraham's seed, and heirs according to the promise.*
>
> (Galatians 3:29)

As heirs of Abraham, we need to acknowledge his example and respond in the same way that he did.

In the Father's house as we gather to praise, worship, and abandon ourselves to His presence we also, as part of our worship, return to Him His tithe. In acknowledgment of the wonderful covenant he has established for us through His Son, Jesus Christ, we partake of the bread and the wine. These two practical expressions of worship were modeled for us by Abraham and we should consider responding the same way as he did.

The Father established a covenant for us and we should respond to Him by putting Him first. Tithing and communion are still very important in the Father's house today and should never be separated because we tithe in response to our covenant relationship with God.

The returned tithe demonstrates that God has first place and that we have put our faith in Him in all areas of our lives. Faith is what pleases the Father. We know that:

> *Without faith it is impossible to please Him, for he who comes to God must believe that He is, and that He is a rewarder of those who diligently seek Him.*
>
> (Hebrews 11:6)

walking in obedience and blessing...

When we return the Father's tithe we come under the same great blessing that Adam and Eve lived under in the Garden of Eden. Part of that blessing was a great intimacy, a wonderful gift of innocence and a freedom of heart to worship unhindered. As I mentioned earlier, the tithe teaches us to put God first. The tithe belongs to God, and we return it in obedience and desire to see Him have first place.

When we return God's tithe, we declare that He is in control of our lives. Through this obedience we have the same opportunity to grow and walk in fellowship with God as Adam and Eve did, and to partake of all the trees in the Garden which are still there to enjoy – including the tree of life.

The tithe returned guarantees blessings that we are not able to contain. The Bible is full of the blessings that God wants to give us, and there is no better place to read about them than in the book of Deuteronomy (New International Version [NIV]):

> *All these blessings will come upon you and accompany you if you obey the Lord your God: You will be blessed in the city and blessed in the country. The fruit of your womb will be blessed,*

and the crops of your land and the young of your livestock — the calves of your herds and the lambs of your flocks. Your basket and your kneading trough will be blessed. You will be blessed when you come in and blessed when you go out. The Lord will grant that the enemies who rise up against you will be defeated before you. They will come at you from one direction but flee from you in seven. The Lord will send a blessing on your barns and on everything you put your hand to. The Lord your God will bless you in the land He is giving you. The Lord will establish you as His holy people, as He promised you on oath, if you keep the command of the Lord your God and walk in His ways. Then all the peoples on earth will see that you are called by the name of the Lord, and they will fear you. The Lord will grant you abundant prosperity — in the fruit of your womb, the young of your livestock and the crops of your ground — in the land He swore to your forefathers to give you. The Lord will open the heavens, the storehouse of His bounty, to send rain on your land in season and to bless all the work of your hands. You will lend to many nations but will borrow from none. The Lord will make you the head, not the tail. If you pay attention to the commands of the Lord your God that I give you this day and carefully follow them, you will always be at the top, never at the bottom.

(Deuteronomy 28:2-13)

father's financial favour

These are some of the great blessings that are poured down on us as we return His tithe! Wherever we live we will be blessed. This includes our children, our enterprises, our food, home and travel. We live under the protection of the Father, for all our enemies have been scattered. Our barns (or in modern terms, our bank accounts or investments) will be blessed.

living under an open heaven ...

In Malachi chapter three we see that the tithe opens the windows of heaven so that blessings are poured down upon us. It is the Father's desire that we walk under an open heaven or under the "smile of God", in the same way that Jesus did when He was baptized:

> *He came up immediately from the water; and behold, the heavens were opened to Him, and He saw the Spirit of God descending like a dove and alighting upon Him.*
>
> (Matthew 3:16)

Jesus lived, walked and ministered for the rest of His life under that open heaven. The heavens did not close over His life until the Father turned His back on Him as He hung on the cross at Golgotha for the sins of the world.

the father's finances

Let's look at an example of this open heaven that Jesus walked under, at a time when he faced a potential financial crisis. At this time, temple tax was being collected, but Jesus had no money with which to make the payment because the disciple Judas (who was responsible for Jesus' ministry finances) had mismanaged the funds that were put into his care. Judas' thieving ways were described by the Apostle John:

> ...this he said, not that he cared for the poor, but because he was a thief, and had the money box; and he used to take what was put in it.
> (John 12:6)

However, Jesus was able to resolve this problem. As we have seen, there was no money to pay the tax that was asked for (Matthew 17:24-27). Because He walked under an open heaven, Jesus saw, by a word of knowledge, a solution to His problem. Jesus was able to see that a fish had a coin in its mouth, so He sent Peter (who was skilled in the art of catching fish) to retrieve the coin.

This story is a wonderful example of situations in the Father's house when we need to rely on each other, and our individual gifts. Jesus had the solution to His problem but He needed someone else in the Father's house to help Him. Jesus was a carpenter and Peter was a fisherman. Both were uniquely talented but totally different in the expression of their God-given gifts.

In the Father's house we all have unique talents and gifts. As we walk under an open heaven we are able to serve and help each other by using our gifts. With our unique gifts, we may be able to bring resolution to situations others face that may be out of their control.

We can all live in this realm of the open heaven. God will show us how, and where, to solve the financial situations which come our way. If we put Him first then the windows of heaven will be opened.

We will see, as Jesus saw, a solution to the financial dilemma that confronts us, and in some cases we may need another gifted person (as Jesus needed Peter) to bring a conclusion to the problem. Father asks us to prove Him in this. Open heaven is a great place to live.

food for the house...

The tithe is also returned *"so that there would be food in my house"* (Malachi 3:10). It is important to understand that as we return the Father's tithe, we bring the release of food to the house. That is, for the preaching of the Word and someone to preach it:

...for the Lord has commanded that those who preach the gospel should live from the gospel.
(1 Corinthians 9:14)

Many people are spiritually starving in an age where there is so much good food (or good teaching) in the body of Christ and this ought not to be so. When we hold back, use or give the Lord's tithe away, and don't return as the Father has asked, there cannot be food in the house of the Lord.

Even though we hear and may even receive the Word (and it may be the most powerful preaching around!), it has no effect on us because we held back that which is not ours to hold back. Proverbs puts it like this – *"one man gives freely, yet gains even more; another withholds unduly, but comes to poverty"* (Proverbs 11:24 NIV).

God has entrusted us with the power of the provision of the food of the house. In other words, the growth, increase and spreading of the gospel from the house. If we trust God and put Him first, then we will trust ourselves to release what is His which is, His tithe and His honor. The power of this trust has been given to every believer.

The growth in our lives can be directly linked to the priority we give to putting God first. We hold the key to spreading the gospel in our area of influence and beyond for we bring the food into the Father's house. If there is no food there is no growth.

If we don't bring the food into the house we can't make a demand on that house for spiritual food. You can sit under the most anointed teachers, and hear the Word straight from heaven, but if you are not bringing His tithe, then there will be no food and your spirit will slowly die.

There can be a house full of food (the Word) but we will have trouble applying or walking in the light of that Word because we are holding back what is rightfully His. As we saw earlier, the writer of Proverbs records that:

> ...there is one who scatters, yet increases more; and there is one who withholds more than is right, but it leads to poverty.
>
> (Proverbs 11:24)

As we respond to the Father in this manner, it protects us from becoming "Judas type" Christians. Judas was the one who betrayed the Lord for thirty pieces of silver. However, his act of betrayal began a long time before this. Judas was close to Jesus. He walked, talked, and ate with the Lord, shared His life and shared in His ministry of miracles, signs and wonders.

As we read earlier, Judas' main ministry (as part

of the twelve chosen by Jesus) was treasurer for the ministry of Jesus. While serving in that capacity he held back what rightly belonged to that ministry and used it for his own ends.

We also have the responsibility of the resources of the Father's house. As sons of the Father, the responsibility has been placed in our hands to release the resources of the ministry of the house (that is, our church). In 1 Corinthians 12:18 we learn that *"God has set the members, each one of them, in the body just as He pleased"*. So we can see that we are set in the body by the Lord, and with this He gives us responsibility for the resources of the house.

The direct flow of food in the house comes from all of us as we return His tithe, for He has set us in the body. When we bring the Father's finances into His house there will always be food in the house, and this action of putting our Father first will protect us financially.

conclusion...

It always brings me great joy when I bring the Father's finances to His house, and especially when I think that as I do this He has found me faithful in returning what is His. I love the Father's promise about faithfulness where his Lord said to him:

Well done, good and faithful servant; you were faithful over a few things, I will make you ruler over many things. Enter into the joy of your Lord.
(Matthew 25:21)

The Father also promises that *"a faithful man will abound with blessings"* (Proverbs 28:20a).

So to summarize, the Father requires us to return to Him a tithe (that is, ten percent of all we earn or are given) in order to:

1. Remind us that all provision comes from God;

2. Give us an opportunity to put God in first place;

3. Remind us that by entrusting to us what is holy and what is His, God is showing us how much He loves us;

4. Give us an opportunity to be found faithful in His sight;

5. Provide us with an opportunity for growth through obedience (as He did for Adam and Eve in the Garden of Eden);

6. Provide food in God's house (Malachi 3). In other words, that there would be someone to preach the Word;

7. And most importantly, that we may walk under an open heaven as Jesus did.

father's financial favour

f

Chapter 3

the father's honour

Thus far we have looked at our Father's house, and His finances. As we saw in the previous chapter, there are guidelines that are set out for us in His Kingdom that help us walk in the blessings of that Kingdom. These guidelines are not formulas to help us get what we can out of the Kingdom, but rather they are patterns that the Father has set out for us in His Word to help us to walk in, and enjoy His Kingdom.

The guideline or principle that will be considered in this chapter is the principle of honor. This involves giving honor where honor is due. This is as outlined for us in Romans where we read that we must:

> *...render therefore to all their due: taxes to whom taxes are due, customs to whom customs, fear to whom fear, honor to whom honor.*
>
> (Romans 13:7)

As we (as the sons of God) return to the Father what is His (that is, the first of all that we are given, earn or inherit) so also should we bring to the Father the honor that is due Him. In the third chapter of the book of Proverbs, we read this wonderful Scripture:

> *My son, do not forget my law, but let your heart keep my commands; for length of days and long life and peace they will add to you. Let not mercy and truth forsake you; bind them around your neck, write them on the tablet of your heart, and so find favor and high esteem in the sight of God and man. Trust in the Lord with all your heart, and lean not on your own understanding; in all your ways acknowledge Him, and He shall direct your paths. Do not be wise in your own eyes; Fear the Lord and depart from evil. It will be health to your flesh, and strength to your bones. Honour the Lord with your possessions and with the first fruits of all your increase; so your barns will be filled with plenty, and your vats will overflow with new wine. My son, do not despise the chastening of the Lord, nor detest His correction; for whom the Lord loves He corrects, just as a father the son in whom*

he delights. Happy is the man who finds wisdom, and the man who gains understanding.
(Proverbs 3:1-13)

The writer of Proverbs exhorts us to honor the Lord. This word "honour" is the Hebrew word "kabad" (*Strong's Concordance* H3513). The primary root of this word is "to be heavy", in other words it means to make things "weighty", or "heavy in favour of". In the context of this discussion, "honour" is used in the sense of making your possessions abound, making them weighty in favor of the Lord.

You will notice that the writer of Proverbs encourages us to bring the firstfruits of all our increase. As we have seen, this is the tithe that demonstrates we are putting God first. However, he also talks about our possessions bringing "honour" to God.

Now, if all we are to do is to return to the Lord what is already His, the question that comes to mind is, what are we giving God? Although returning the tithe does wonderful things for us, how then do we bring honor to the Father? The answer is simple. What brings Him honor is when we bring to Him an offering from that which we have to live and enjoy life with, that is, our substance or possessions.

In the Father's house there is great blessing for us as we return His tithe. However, we also see in

father's financial favour

Proverbs that God receives honor when we bring Him an offering from our substance. God's heart's cry to His people was for them to honor Him, and as they did so, honor would return to them.

It is the Father's desire that His children would live in a place of honor, but for that to happen they have to first honor Him. In Malachi we see the Father's cry for the order of things in His Kingdom:

> ...a son honours his father and a servant his master. If then I am the Father, where is my honour? And if I am a Master, where is my reverence? says the Lord of hosts.
>
> (Malachi 1:6)

When God brought an accusation against His people Israel, He said:

> Will a man rob God? Yet you have robbed Me! But you say, 'In what way have we robbed You?' In tithes and offerings. You are cursed with a curse, for you have robbed Me, even this whole nation. Bring all the tithes into the storehouse, that there may be food in my house, and try Me now in this, says the Lord of hosts, if I will not open for you the windows of heaven and pour out for you such blessing that there will not be room enough to receive it.
>
> (Malachi 3:8-10)

One of the very sad things I have discovered as I have traveled around the world is the fact that so many Christians believe their whole responsibility to God and His financial order is the tithe, and the tithe alone – as if the tithe is some a sort of panacea. The unfortunate thing about this is that they miss out on so much of the blessing that the Father wants to give.

In the Father's house our responsibility goes much deeper that just the tithe. We are asked to honor the Father with our substance, and to respond to Father the way He wants us to does cost us something. To truly honor someone it must come out of a relationship of deep love and caring. As we respond, the cost of the honor is far outweighed by the value of giving the honor. The book of Proverbs says we should give to the Father of our substance (in other words, the offering) which is honor or worship and we should give the firstfruit (the tithe) which is an act of faith and puts God in first place.

The honor that is asked for in Proverbs is an offering from that which we have left over after we return the Lord's tithe. As you read through the entire Bible you will discover that the Lord loves offerings.

In chapter twenty two of Genesis we read an

account of God asking Abraham for an offering, specifically a burnt offering. The definition of a burnt offering is "not...literally 'burnt offering' but what is brought up or presented to the Deity. The name is a translation of the Septuagint rendering, which is itself based upon the descriptive phrase often attached to 'olah' in the ritual prescriptions: 'an offering made by fire unto the Lord'. The burnt offering was the highest order of sacrifice in the Old Testament ritual" (Morris Jastrow Jr.).

So Abraham was asked by God for an offering, and not just any offering but a complete offering. We have already established in previous chapters the wonderful relationship that Abraham had with the Father, and now his heart is exposed again for all to see just how deep this relationship really was. When I read this account, I am left in no doubt as to how much Abraham loved the Father, and how his response declared the depths of his trust in the nature and the character of God. Notice Abraham's response when he said to his young men:

> *Stay here with the donkey; the lad and I will go yonder and worship, and we will come back to you.*
>
> (Genesis 22:5)

As Abraham responded to God, he took the substance (that is, his offering) up to the top of the mountain to worship God. It was truly a complete and whole offering, and he was prepared to allow the fire he would build to consume the offering. What Abraham was prepared to do for God was to lay his dreams, his future, and all the promises that God had given to him on the fire of the altar as his worship to God.

The reality was that Abraham was more interested in worshipping God than he was in the promises of God that he had been given. He responded in obedience to God because at the very heart of Abraham was the principle of putting God first. His worship was his offering.

Every day we have to make a similar choice – to put God first or to put ourselves first. We can choose to just trust God or to find our own solutions to situations that we face. The choices before each of us will sway us to either bend our principles to conform to our actions, or bend our actions to conform to our principles. Every day we have to face decisions to put God first.

As we have seen, the writer of Proverbs says we are to honor the Lord with our substance. Abraham honored the Lord with his offering. Today there is much confusion in the Father's house about this simple principle of honoring the Father with our substance, which both honors Him and becomes an offering unto Him.

When God needed a place to dwell with His people Israel in the wilderness, He spoke to Moses and gave him instructions concerning what He wanted him to do:

> *Take from among you an offering to the Lord. Whoever is of a willing heart, let him bring it as an offering to the Lord: gold, silver, and bronze; blue, purple, and scarlet thread, fine linen, and goats' hair; ram skins dyed red, badger skins, and acacia wood; oil for the light, and spices for the anointing oil and for the sweet incense; onyx stones, and stones to be set in the ephod and in the breastplate. All who are gifted artisans among you shall come and make all that the Lord has commanded.*
>
> (Exodus 35:5-10)

All these things that God asked for (such as the gold, silver and bronze, the blue and purple thread) were all the things that He had obtained for them as they were leaving Egypt after four hundred years of slavery. The purpose of these precious things was not to meet their needs in the wilderness. Rather, their food, water, clothing and shelter were supplied or maintained by God on a daily basis, over and above what they had brought with them out of Egypt.

the father's honour

The book of Psalms (Psalm 105) records that God brought them out with silver and gold, there were no feeble people and He gave a cloud for a covering, and fire to give light in the night. He brought quail to them when they asked, and satisfied them with the bread of heaven. When they were thirsty, water ran in dry places from the rock.

God asked Moses to build a dwelling place for His presence according to the pattern of what is in heaven. He asked His people to honor Him with an offering from the substance that He had provided. You will notice that the instructions were for those who were of a willing heart. This is so important for us to take hold of, because God always loves a willing heart. He loves cheerful givers, those who desire to honor Him from the substance which He has already provided.

So, when I talk about an offering, I am talking about it in the same context as the writer in Proverbs, who told us to honor the Lord with our substance. In other words, the offering is to come from our possessions, and is not part of God's tithe. As we saw earlier, a son honors his father and a servant his master. In the same way, God says to us *"If I am the Father, where is My honor?"*

The confusion arises among the sons of the house

when they are presented with opportunities to give to multiple "offerings". These include collections for visiting ministry, the poor, the building fund, the missionary vision of the church, and any other project that the church may have on at the time. All of these projects are not wrong in themselves, and are all things that the church should be doing and be doing them as unto the Lord. However, my question is, "Should all the above mentioned things be called 'offerings'?"

The Oxford Dictionary definition of "offering" is to "present ... to a deity". In other words, an offering is given directly to God, from the heart, with no designation – not via some program or ministry where its use has already been determined.

Some confusion has also arisen in relation to receiving the tithe in the Father's house, where traditionally this has also been called an offering. We know now that the tithe can never be an offering because an offering comes from the resources that the Father has supplied to us. The tithe, on the other hand, always belongs to the Father and is never given or offered, but always returned. Whenever confusion exists about what constitutes an offering, the sons of the house are losing the opportunity to honor the Father.

A safe and balanced approach I would like to suggest is for us first to understand from Scripture (in both the Old and the New Testaments) that the Word declares very loudly that offerings are always upward and never sideways. Put another way, an offering is always vertical, never horizontal. The offering has the same place as worship – it is always God-focused, never man-focused. Of all the offerings that are recorded in the Word, the one that I love the most is the burnt offering. The reason for this is that there can be no doubt as to the destination of the offering, for it was consumed by the fire as worship to God.

When I am talking about an offering to the Father – His offering, His honor – I am not referring to missions, or the poor, or the building fund. I am not referring to mercy or a love gift for someone, nor am I talking about planting or sowing seeds so that I may receive a harvest. These are all things we should be doing because they are part of our Christian lifestyle, and as already mentioned, should be done as unto the Lord. They are our Christian responsibility, in other words, our commitment and Christian service to and for the Kingdom of God, for freely we have received and freely we give.

However, in the sense of the Father's honor, none of the acts mentioned in the previous paragraph constitute an offering, even though they have been traditionally labeled as offerings in the church. An offering is that which is given directly to God, from the heart, with no purpose other than His honor. In the next chapter the subject of our Christian responsibilities will be covered in more detail.

Leaders must be careful that they do not do an injustice to the sons of the house when they are receiving offerings. The need to retain integrity is paramount in this area of Christian service, for it is the leader's job to take the people deeper into freedoms that are there for all the sons of the house, especially in this area of finances.

It is very important that there is an understanding of the terminology that is being used and its meaning so that we don't simply label all that is given or all that has been asked for as an "offering". The Father takes His offering seriously and we should do the same.

In Genesis chapter four, we read the story of Cain and Abel. It is recorded that when Abel approached God, he brought the firstfruit of his lambs, which as we have already discovered was the tithe, but he did not stop at this act of obedience (or faith). He did much more than that. The Bible records that he also brought the fat and that *"the Lord respected Abel and his offering"* (Genesis 4:4).

The fat was the part that was highly prized. It belonged to Abel and he could do with it as he pleased, but instead he came and honored the Lord with it. So Abel brought not just the firstfruit to God, but he also brought the fat, that is, he brought the offering, or the substance. The Bible records that as a result of this, the Lord respected Abel.

In this same account in Genesis, Cain (who was Abel's brother) also brought the firstfruits, however this was not respected by God in the same way that Abel's offering was accepted. Both Cain and Abel approached God with the fruit of their labor, so why did God accept one and reject the other?

Now there are many books and articles which deal with this question, and much has been written about the lamb offering that was presented to God. I don't want to add to, or take away from all this great teaching. Instead, what I would like the reader to focus on is the difference in the approach to God that the two brothers had.

The Bible says that "in the process of time Cain brought an offering of the *"firstfruit of the ground"* (Genesis 4:3). It is worth noting at this time that the Bible does not recall that Cain added anything to the firstfruit he brought. This is in contrast to Abel, who

father's financial favour

first brought the firstfruits of his flock, and then added the fat (in other words, the offering). We have already seen that the firstfruit declares that Father has first place, whereas the offering honors the Father.

What we see here is that one brother's approach with an offering was respected by God, and the other's was rejected. I would like to suggest that the reason for this was that what Cain presented to God was not based on a heart attitude of honor, but of duty. In other words, he presented "in the process of time" (that is, in his time) the firstfruits of the ground (or tithe) but did not add any honor. Whereas, Abel gave to God the fat of the lambs, which was his to do with as he liked, and God respected his offering.

Putting God in first place is a choice we have to make every day. How can we honor Him with an offering, if in our hearts we have not put Him in first place? With Cain the problem was with the attitude of his heart. Father said to him:

> *If you do well, will you not be accepted? And if you do not do well, sin lies at the door. And its desire is for you, but you should rule over it.*
>
> (Genesis 4:7)

What an awesome thing to be respected by the Father as Abel was and to have Him respect that which you honored Him with. In the Father's house everything we do must spring from a heart that wants to put the Father first. So when we come into His house and bring to Him His tithe, we should remember the need to honor Him and we do that with an offering from our substance.

What I would like to suggest to the reader is this simple thing: when we come into the Father's house and return to Him that which is His (that is, the tithe), then we should also take some time to ask Him what He would like as an offering. Something like "Father, here is Your firstfruit, what would You like as an offering this morning, what is Your honor?"

The wonderful thing about this sort of prayer or this heart attitude toward the Father is that there will not be any lack. There will never be any shortfall in the resources that you have because He will always provide for that which He asks for.

As we have seen, Abraham knew that God would provide for the offering and he told Isaac:

> *'My son, God will provide for Himself the lamb for a burnt offering', so the two of them went together.*
> (Genesis 22:8)

Keep foremost in your mind this simple thing – all

the gold and the silver belongs to the Lord (Haggai 2:8) so whatever we have, and whatever He asks for, is already supplied by Him.

Chapter Four

the father's expectation

Within every financial structure, there are certain expectations that are placed on those who use that structure, in order for it to work to its maximum efficiency. Similarly, the Kingdom of God places certain expectations on those who live in the freedom of its covering. In other words, there is financial order in the Father's Kingdom and as sons living in this Kingdom there are expectations placed on our lives.

One of those expectations is that we should be about the Father's business, that is, the extension of the Kingdom of God. Once we accept this, the question that often comes to mind is how to do it? Because this book is written from a financial point of

father's financial favour

view, I will present our responsibilities within a financial framework.

In this chapter I trust that we can obtain an understanding of the Father's expectations of us, remembering that, as His sons, we have His favor on our lives and everything we have is provided by Him.

Now it is not unrealistic to expect that if someone is living at home with their parents, that their earthly father would have expectations regarding their behavior and what is accepted in the home (for example, paying a financial contribution towards food and board). In the same way, there are a number of things our heavenly Father expects of the sons of the house. I like to call these expectations "Christian Responsibilities".

These responsibilities encompass a number of areas of the Kingdom, including missions, mercy, ministry and management. Each one of these areas require a financial commitment in order to accomplish the Father's goals. The wonderful thing about having these responsibilities entrusted to us is that we get to share the resources that the Father has given us with others, and we have the incredible privilege of helping to extend the Kingdom of God.

the father's expectation

There is one point that needs to be clarified before we approach the different responsibilities that are there for us. I believe it is important to understand that the financial expectations the Father has for our lives are not those that come under the umbrella of offerings that are received in the Father's house. As we have already discovered in the previous chapter, we bring offerings to the Father because we have a relationship with Him and want to bring honor to Him. In other words, the action of bringing an offering demonstrates our love for the Father, whereas the financial expectations He has for us relate to the administrative responsibilities we have as sons living in His house.

I am of the firm opinion that if we address the expectations of the Father as our Christian responsibility, then we will manage the resources that God has given us with greater stewardship. It is important to remember that:

> ...as many as received Him, to them He gave the right to become children of God, to those who believe in His name.
> (John 1:12)

This brings with it certain responsibilities both to the Father, in terms of the return of the Father's tithe and offerings into His house, and also to other people.

father's financial favour

Jesus outlined our responsibility to:

...love the Lord your God with all your heart, with all your soul, with all your strength, and with all your mind, and your neighbour as yourself.

(Luke 10:27)

As I stated earlier, church leaders must be very mindful that they do not teach those whom the Holy Spirit has given them charge over that our Christian responsibilities are met by the offerings that are received in the church. If all financial contributions are categorized as "offerings", it implies that they are also a matter of choice and if they are a matter of choice the danger is that it would undermine the need to take up the responsibilities of the house that are ours as sons.

To illustrate, if we "choose" not to pay board to our earthly father, it impacts on the effective running of the house, and the others who live in it. So if we teach that all offerings must be God-ward, then we have then to look at a different paradigm for fulfilling our responsibility to our fellow man.

I love the way Jesus put it as a twelve-year-old boy, when he asked His parents:

Why did you seek Me? Did you not know that I

must be about My Father's business?
(Luke 2:24)

I believe the "business" He was referring to was our responsibility to our fellow man, which takes the forms of missions, mercy, ministry and management. Therefore, when we acknowledge that the Father is to be first, as His sons we should view these four areas of responsibility as nonnegotiable for our lives. We will now look at these four areas in more detail.

responsibility for missions...

Our first area of responsibility is to finance the work of missions. In my travels throughout the world it has been very interesting to listen to the approach that many Christians have towards their responsibility for missions. The most popular response seems to be that, for many, giving to missions means giving resources to whoever tugs on their heart strings the most.

For some, the release of finances to missions is governed by what they want to do and the way that they want to do it. In other words, they see the need to have a say in how their contributions are spent. For others, it is a solemn yet wonderful privilege to get behind what their local church is doing. It is the latter that I believe is the most effective method for achieving the Father's goals, and therefore the one most church members should adopt.

The Word of God teaches us that:

> *God has set the members, each one of them, in the body just as He pleased.*
>
> (1 Corinthians 12:18)

Therefore, if we have been set by God in the body which is the church we attend, He has specific reasons for placing us there. One of these reasons is to support the Godly vision He gave to that particular church in order to touch a dying world with the gospel. This task is accomplished not only with our prayer and our time, but with the financial resources that the Father has put at our disposal.

We also need to keep in mind that the call of missions is not restricted to overseas destinations. "Missions" has a much broader scope. The Apostle Paul explained it very succinctly, that:

> *...you shall receive power when the Holy Spirit has come upon you; and you shall be witnesses to Me in Jerusalem, and in all Judea and Samaria, and to the end of the earth.*
>
> (Acts 1:8)

At this point, you may be asking yourself what

Jerusalem, Judea and Samaria mean to us today, so I will explain the order that has been set out here for us in this chapter of the book of Acts.

I believe that for us, Jerusalem refers to those who are in the local governmental area in which our church is situated. This is the area where we live, and do business, and so the proof of the gospel can be seen operating in our lives. Therefore, I would suggest that this is the first area of responsibility that we should give resources to.

The next area mentioned in this chapter of Acts is Judea, which was the greater surrounding area of the city of Jerusalem. I believe that in today's context this refers to the state or territory that your city is located in.

The third area mentioned is Samaria. In the time of Jesus, the Samaritans were a group of people who were loathed by the Jewish people of the day. When Jesus met the Samaritan woman at the well she asked Him:

> ...how is it that you, being a Jew, ask a drink from me, a Samaritan woman? For Jews have no dealings with Samaritans.
>
> (John 4:9)

So, while Samaria was a region, I believe it has

more to do with a group of people than a geographical place or territory, and therefore is the most challenging area of missions for us today.

Who are considered the "despised" group of people in our generation who live not too far from us? What group or groups of people do we as Christians have a hard time relating to, or are even a little afraid of, because of their lifestyles or beliefs? I will leave that for you to answer as an individual, but consider that these people may be the Samaritans of our day.

The final location mentioned in this passage in Acts is "the end of the earth". This encompasses every nation and tongue that the Lord impresses on the local church to reach, and it behooves the local church to do all that it can with the resources it is given to reach these areas and demonstrate the gospel of Jesus Christ.

As far as missions are concerned, the key to fulfilling our responsibility to the Father is that we do not run off with our own visions of missions, releasing resources that the Father would rather use in and through the church where He has planted us. It is the Father's desire that His sons would be a people who would not want to control, but would be willing and grateful stewards of the resources He has allocated for their church.

A spirit of control is detrimental to the work of missions. It is only with commitment to a single purpose that we will achieve all that He has reserved for our church. As we keep this sort of heart attitude toward the resources that He has placed in our hands, then we can be assured He will give us more resources to extend His Kingdom further because as we discussed earlier, it is our attitude toward giving that is most important to the Father.

Finally, missions are the responsibility of all in the church. Jesus told us to:

> ...heal the sick, cleanse the lepers, raise the dead, cast out demons. Freely you have received, freely give.
> (Matthew 10:8)

responsibility for mercy . . .

The next responsibility that we have in the Father's house is the responsibility of mercy. As this is obviously a large subject I will, as before, keep within the confines of financial management.

The major characteristic of mercy is that it involves the poor. Jesus told us that *"blessed are the merciful, for they shall obtain mercy"* (Matthew 5:7).

father's financial favour

When we show love, kindness and mercy to someone less fortunate than ourselves, we set off a reaction that has eternal ramifications both for us and our loved ones, because the poor have a special place in the heart of God.

In the book of Leviticus we see that God gave special instructions to the land owners at harvest time with regard to the poor, telling them:

> *When you reap the harvest of your land, you shall not wholly reap the corners of your field, nor shall you gather the gleanings of your harvest. And you shall not glean your vineyard, nor shall you gather every grape of your vineyard; you shall leave them for the poor and the stranger: I am the Lord your God.*
>
> (Leviticus 19:9-10)

Right from the very beginning of the time of Israel (that is, the people of God), we find that God was showing His people that they are responsible for the poor. He made provision for those who were less fortunate than others, and instructed the people:

> *If there is among you a poor man of your brethren, within any of the gates in your land which the Lord your God is giving you, you shall not harden your heart nor shut your hand from your poor brother, but you shall open your hand wide to him*

and willingly lend him sufficient for his need, whatever he needs.
(Deuteronomy 15:7-8)

It is the heart of the Father that the poor are looked after, and the Old Testament is full of instructions to the people of God concerning their attitude and actions in dealing with these people. The Old Testament also outlines the great blessings that are bestowed on those who take these instructions seriously. The Psalmist records that:

...blessed is he who considers the poor; The Lord will deliver him in time of trouble.
(Psalm 41:1)

In fact, in the Father's house there is a responsibility on the sons of the house to not only just "consider" (or think about) the poor, but to pour out their lives and resources for them.

If the sons of the house would realize the blessing that flows on to them and their families as a result of this, then I believe there would be no shortage of resources available to fulfill this responsibility, because we are told that:

...he who has pity on the poor lends to the Lord, and He will pay back what he has given.
(Proverbs 19:17)

When Jesus began His ministry here on earth, He quoted a verse from Isaiah, saying:

> *The Spirit of the Lord is upon Me, Because He has anointed Me to preach the gospel to the poor; He has sent Me to heal the broken-hearted, To proclaim liberty to the captives and recovery of sight to the blind, To set at liberty those who are oppressed.*
>
> (Luke 4:19)

It is very interesting to note the order in which the Holy Spirit wanted this written – Jesus said the Spirit of God was upon Him first so that He could preach the good news to the poor.

As you study the life and ministry of Jesus, it seems that this was a priority for Him. If we take Jesus' life as our standard, then this should also be a priority for our own life and ministry. So what exactly is this "good news to the poor" of which Jesus spoke?

From a Christian perspective, the most common answer would probably be that it refers to the sharing of the gospel, that is, telling the poor about the death and resurrection of Jesus and all the great benefits that arise from that. As wonderful as this is, I wonder whether from a poor person's perspective, "good news" would mean there was to be food on the table (providing they even have a table!), or that they were starting a job that would promote their self esteem or teach them to provide for their families.

In other words, instead of just talking about the love of Jesus, we should be demonstrating it as well through the provision of resources and teaching of life skills. I believe this is "good news" for the poor. We can't leave the gospel message untold. However, we need to remember that:

> ...whoever has this world's goods, and sees his brother in need, and shuts up his heart from him, how does the love of God abide in him?
>
> (1 John 3:17)

Much of what Jesus shared with the disciples and the people of His day had to do with the poor. It is significant that He told them that it would be the poor who would inherit the Kingdom of God. In the book of Luke, chapter eighteen, we read a wonderful story about a ruler who, when he was challenged by Jesus, seemed to struggle with the notion of giving to the poor.

This story has often resulted in rich people feeling condemned by others because of the abundance of resources that they have at their disposal. If we have taken this stand then we may have missed a

father's financial favour

wonderful truth in this passage. A certain ruler asked Jesus, saying:

> *Good Teacher, what shall I do to inherit eternal life? You know the commandments: 'Do not commit adultery,' 'Do not murder,' 'Do not steal,' 'Do not bear false witness,' 'Honor your father and your mother.' And he said all these things I have kept from my youth. So when Jesus heard these things, He said to him, you still lack one thing. Sell all that you have and distribute to the poor and you will have treasure in heaven; and come, follow Me. But when he heard this, he became very sorrowful, for he was very rich. And when Jesus saw that he became very sorrowful, He said, how hard it is for those who have riches to enter the kingdom of God! For it is easier for a camel to go through the eye of a needle than for a rich man to enter the kingdom of God. And those who heard it said who then can be saved? But He said the things which are impossible with men are possible with God.*
>
> (Luke 18:18-27)

Jesus responds to this genuine approach from the ruler who wanted to inherit eternal life and asks him about the commandments that relate to his fellow man (such as 'Do not commit adultery,' 'Do not murder,' 'Do not steal,' 'Do not bear false witness,' 'Honour your father and your mother'). The ruler replied that he had kept them from his youth. Jesus replies with the statement that there is "one thing you still lack".

Here Jesus gives us all a very important key. We can keep all these commandments that relate to our relationship with our fellow man, but still miss the area that God wants us to take special note of, that is, the poor.

There is a responsibility placed on those who know Him and are known by Him to follow after His heart, which is to bring good news to the poor. The prophet Isaiah tells us:

> ...how beautiful upon the mountains are the feet of him who brings good news, who proclaims peace, who brings glad tidings of good things, who proclaims salvation, who says to Zion, Your God reigns!
>
> (Isaiah 52:7)

Please understand that Jesus was not in any way after the ruler's money. Rather, He was after his heart. However, the ruler's heart was a long way from the poor, and what he did not realize was that if he had given his goods to the poor, then the goods would have been returned to him.

The ruler may have kept the commands according to his confession, but it is apparent he did not know the heart of God. Had he known, he would have understood that *"he who has pity on the poor lends to the Lord, and He will pay back what he has given"* (Proverbs 19:17).

In contrast to this story, in Luke (chapter 19) we read that Jesus told Zacchaeus that salvation had come to his house. Part of the reason for this was that Jesus saw the fruit of salvation in Zacchaeus from the fact that he gave half his goods to the poor.

When we respond to the responsibilities of the Father's house and make the poor a priority, there is another important principle that we need to consider. This is a principle that comes from the very heart of God and this Scripture explains it best:

> *Take heed that you do not do your charitable deeds before men, to be seen by them. Otherwise you have no reward from your Father in heaven. Therefore, when you do a charitable deed, do not sound a trumpet before you as the hypocrites do in the synagogues and in the streets, that they may have glory from men. Assuredly, I say to you, they have their reward. But when you do a charitable deed, do not let your left hand know what your right hand is doing, that your charitable deed may be in secret; and your Father who sees in secret will Himself reward you openly.*
>
> (Matthew 6:1-4)

It is the Father's heart that we would bless the poor in secret. It helps them to realize that God has their best interests at heart, and allows them to have dignity about their lives. There is no greater joy than to see a person less fortunate receive a gift from someone they will never know and never be indebted to. The freedom that this act generates is a wonder to see.

There is no doubt according to Scripture that it is our responsibility as individual believers to help the poor, and that the reward will come from the Father as we do our acts of kindness in secret. When you keep these acts that the Father requires known only to yourself, there will always be a reward, because it engenders faith and trust in us and allows us not to be robbed.

If you take the words of Jesus seriously, you will discover that not only will the poor be blessed, but there will always be more resources to do what the Father wants done. God is:

> ...*able to make all grace abound toward you, that you, always having all sufficiency in all things, may have abundance for every good work.*
> (2 Corinthians 9:8)

He will get it to you, if He can get it through you!

responsibility for ministry . . .

The next area of responsibility that we need to take seriously as sons of the Father's house has to do with the area of ministry. When I use the word "ministry" I'm not so much talking about the particular ministry gift which we have been given, I am referring more to the very important task of ministering to the servants of the Lord.

Realistically, not many of us will be in a position to lay hands on these servants and bless them directly. However, we can all minister in another important way, which is to provide for their needs. The Apostle Paul asked:

> *If we have sown spiritual things for you, is it a great thing if we reap your material things?*
> (1 Corinthians 9:11)

It is the heart of the Father that those who minister for Him would have their needs provided by those they minister to.

The writer of Ephesians tells us that when Jesus ascended, *"He led captivity captive, and gave gifts to men"* (Ephesians 4:8). We learn that these gifts are for:

> ...some to be apostles, some prophets, some evangelists, and some pastors and teachers, for the equipping of the saints for the work of ministry, for the edifying of the body of Christ.
> (Ephesians 4:11)

So we see that the servants of the Lord are gifts to us, and therefore we need to value them. One way we can do this is by honoring them with love gifts and providing for their needs.

The wonderful thing about honoring these servants or "gifts" that are amongst us is that honor returns to us. Matthew explains that:

> ...he who receives a prophet in the name of a prophet shall receive a prophet's reward. And he who receives a righteous man in the name of a righteous man shall receive a righteous man's reward.
> (Matthew 10:41)

In other words, rather than just acknowledging them, we should receive them, that is, bless them and attend to them as gifts given to us. When we do this, then we also receive in full.

Jesus outlined the principle for providing for the servants of the Lord. In the gospel of Mark we read that Jesus:

> ...called the twelve to Himself, and began to send

> *them out two by two, and gave them power over unclean spirits. He commanded them to take nothing for the journey except a staff; no bag, no bread, no copper in their money belts; but to wear sandals, and not to put on two tunics. Also He said to them, in whatever place you enter a house, stay there till you depart from that place. And whoever will not receive you nor hear you, when you depart from there, shake off the dust under your feet as a testimony against them.*
>
> (Mark 6:7-10)

As you look at this Scripture, you can see that it was Jesus' expectation that it was the people to whom the disciples ministered that would provide for all their needs. I believe that the same principle applies today. We have a responsibility to look out for, and minister to, the needs of those who serve the Lord and by service to the sons of God.

The call of the servants of God is:

> *...for the equipping of the saints for the work of ministry, for the edifying of the body of Christ, until we all come to the unity of the faith and of the knowledge of the Son of God, to a perfect man, to the measure of the stature of the fullness of Christ.*
>
> (Ephesians 4:12-13)

The Bible is very clear about our responsibility in this matter:

Do you not know that those who minister the holy things eat of the things of the temple, and those who serve at the altar partake of the offerings of the altar? Even so the Lord has commanded that those who preach the gospel should live from the gospel.

(1 Corinthians 9:13-14)

In many cases, the servants of the Lord have made great sacrifices for, and on behalf of, the sons of the Father's house and it is a small thing that we should sacrifice some of what God has given to us to make their lives a little easier.

There is a principle of honor that I think we also need to apply to the servants of the Lord. We are to make sure that:

...the elders who rule well be counted worthy of double honor, especially those who labor in the word and doctrine. For the Scripture says, you shall not muzzle an ox while it treads out the grain and the labourer is worthy of his wages.

(1 Timothy 5:17-18)

In Ephesians we are told to honor our father and mother, which is the first commandment with a promise attached to it – *"that it may be well with you and you may live long on the earth"* (Ephesians 6:2-3). We are also told to:

father's financial favour

...obey those who rule over you, and be submissive, for they watch out for your souls, as those who must give account. Let them do so with joy and not with grief, for that would be unprofitable for you.
(Hebrews 13:17)

So we see from these scriptures that as we honor and minister to the servants of the Lord, this honor returns to us in the form of long life and well-being.

If we understand that we are responsible for ministering to the servants of the Lord, our next question would most likely be "how should we support them?" We discovered in a previous chapter that we are to bring the Lord's tithe into the house so that there may be food. This then, is what in most cases provides a basic living for the servants of the Lord in that house.

However, in some cases there may not be sufficient resources to do this because the house (that is, the church) does not have enough members to provide a wage. In these cases, the servants of the Lord may have to accept external employment for a season in order to support their families.

It is imperative that we understand that when we return the Lord's tithe that our responsibility to the house is not over. We also have responsibility for the ongoing well-being of those who minister to the sons of God. We are to meet this responsibility from the abundance that we have left over after our own needs have been met.

The Bible tells us that God gives bread for food and seed for sowing (2 Corinthians 9:10). God provides for all that we need (that is, bread for food) and He also gives the ability to reap a harvest (that is, seed for sowing). This subject of the seed and the harvest will be covered in the next chapter.

So to summarize, our harvest or our abundance should be used to help others, especially those who minister as the servants of God. The Apostle Paul tells us that:

> ...by an equality, that now at this time your abundance may supply their lack, that their abundance also may supply your lack that there may be equality.
>
> (2 Corinthians 8:14)

In other words, we must first have a willing mind.

We need to see that it is our responsibility and accept with joy the fact that God has given us a part to play in their ministries. As we respond to God and our responsibilities, He is:

> ...able to make all grace abound toward you, that you, always having all sufficiency in all things,

may have an abundance for every good work.
(2 Corinthians 9:8)

responsibility for management...

The next responsibility that we need to look at in the Father's house is the area of management. I use the word "management" in the context of being a good steward of the resources that the Father has placed in our hands, in order to fulfill the responsibilities that are ours as sons of the Father's house.

In most of the Christian world, church services are held in buildings that are either rented or owned outright by the church. I like to call these places the Father's house. The question that people often raise is, "Who has the responsibility for these buildings and how should this responsibility be met?"

If you are in a church where the building is totally debt free then you are truly blessed; however, there is still a need for you to understand that from time to time building-related issues will arise (such as maintenance, or the ongoing vision to build a bigger facility), and that these issues require funds. There will never be a shortage of funds for these things when the sons of the house realize that it is their responsibility.

These are not things that are to be funded by the return of the Lord's tithe, but from the resources that the Father has placed in our hands. As we know, the tithe is for food – the ongoing spiritual well-being of the Father's house. The practical well-being of the Father's house is to be supplied by those who use it.

In the book of Nehemiah there is a wonderful Scripture that deals with the natural and the spiritual, working side by side to rebuild the wall. Nehemiah tells us that:

> ...those who built on the wall, and those who carried burdens, loaded themselves so that with one hand they worked at construction, and with the other held a weapon. Every one of the builders had his sword girded at his side as he built. And the one who sounded the trumpet was beside me.
> (Nehemiah 4:17-18)

Here we see the sword and the shovel side by side.

We find that when Nehemiah was building the walls, not only did he labor, but he also had his sword at the ready. In other words, while it is good to wave our spiritual swords around and do all the spiritual things that are required, such as bringing the Lord's tithe and offering into His storehouse, it is not the only thing.

father's financial favour

We still have many practical things that need to be accomplished as with any house. We can pray and ask God for all that we need to build or buy a building, which is important, and is what most Christians do. However, the reality is that someone has to pick up the shovel and do something. Just as the spiritual provision has been taken care of, the practical must also be addressed because faith and works go together.

To accept responsibility for the house we have to have a willing heart – another important point to consider if you are part of the Father's house in a building that is rented rather than owned by the church. The church rent should never be paid for with the money that comes in for spiritual food (that is, the tithe).

We would never make a practice of paying rent on our residential house with the money we needed to buy the food with. We must apply the same rule in the Father's house. If we continue to use the food money to pay for the building we use to hold church, there will come a day when the food will stop and there will be spiritual hunger in the house.

As children grow up in the family home, become adults and earn a living, they take on some of the responsibilities of the house in which they live. That

the father's expectation

is assuming, of course, that they are being raised by parents who see the need to prepare them for life and are training them to become responsible citizens. Remember, *"a good man leaves an inheritance to his children's children"* (Proverbs 13:22a).

This same principle of "those who use the house pay for the house" applies in the church. If the rent has to be paid, then the sons of the house who use that building have the responsibility to meet this need (remember "sons" is a non-gender term for those who come into the inheritance). They should take the time to ask the Father what their level of responsibility should be to the house in monetary terms.

Even though, we read through Scripture that God had places of habitation:

> *I have heard your prayer and your supplication that you have made before Me; I have consecrated this house which you have built to put My name there forever, and My eyes and My heart will be there perpetually.*
>
> (1 Kings 9:3)

We know, of course, that no space we rent or build can in any way, shape or form contain the living God, for He cannot be held into one particular area.

father's financial favour

From a practical point we know that we as individuals all carry the presence of God. The Apostle Paul tells us that:

> ...to them God willed to make known what are the riches of the glory of this mystery among the Gentiles: which is Christ in you, the hope of glory.
> (Colossians 1:27)

In this way we see that the house we come into collectively to worship God (the Father's house) is also for His divine presence. Notice that Paul also says:

> ...but if all prophesy, and an unbeliever or an uninformed person comes in, he is convinced by all, he is convicted by all, and thus the secrets of his heart are revealed and so, falling down on his face, he will worship God and report that God is truly among you.
> (1 Corinthians 14:24-25)

The message that the prophet Haggai brought to the people of God had to do with them taking up responsibility for the Father's house. God takes this seriously, and we should do no less:

> Now therefore, thus says the Lord of hosts: 'consider your ways! You have sown much, and bring in little; You eat, but do not have enough; You drink, but you are not filled with drink; You clothe yourselves, but

no one is warm; And he who earns wages, Earns wages to put into a bag with holes. Thus says the Lord of hosts 'Consider your ways!' Go up to the mountains and bring wood and build the temple that I may take pleasure in it and be glorified' says the Lord. You looked for much, but indeed it came to little; and when you brought it home, I blew it away. Why? says the Lord of hosts. 'Because of My house that is in ruins, while every one of you runs to his own house.'

(Haggai 1:5-9)

The management of the Father's house is the responsibility of all that use it. A willing heart is what is required. The Psalmist believed that:

...a day in your courts is better than a thousand. I would rather be a doorkeeper in the house of my God than dwell in the tents of wickedness.

(Psalm 84:10)

This responsibility, this willing heart, has nothing to do with what we do or do not have. It's not about the economy – it' about confidence in God, in God's design for us as a Church, in God's ability! It is in knowing that He is a God who is very interested in the generations that are yet to come. We take responsibility because we want a secure future for these generations. We must be like the

Psalmist who said:

> *I will not give sleep to my eyes or slumber to my eyelids, until I find a place for the Lord, a dwelling place for the Mighty One of Jacob.*
>
> (Psalm 132:4-5)

In summary, the tithe is for the food in the Father's house. The offerings are for honor in the Fathers house. Although traditionally all the funds that were received to provide for the areas of missions, mercy, ministry or management were called offerings, these are our Christian responsibilities as sons of the Father's house and are the expectations of the Father for our lives.

Chapter 5

the father's favour

The subject matter of this chapter is so important for our hearts and minds to understand, for so many sons in the Father's house think that He has held something back from them. They think that somehow they have to "guts it out" and just survive financially while many others seem to be living in incredible blessing.

Please understand that the favor of the Father is for all, and the reason that it may not have manifested in so many people's lives is not because Father is holding back – because even the ungrateful and wicked are receivers of His kindness (Luke 6:35).

In fact, the reason is because there is so much misunderstanding about the Father's financial favor. Notice that the Apostle Paul says that:

> *God is able to make all grace abound toward you, that you, always having all sufficiency in all things, may have an abundance for every good work.*
>
> (2 Corinthians 9:8)

Paul uses some very inclusive words in this passage of Scripture. He uses the words "all grace" not "some grace" to emphasize that there is no limit to the financial grace that God can pour into your life.

This is one of the important lessons to learn about the nature of God. He holds nothing back from us, His sons. If you are feeling that He is holding back from you, let me encourage you with the fact that this is not in His nature. If you stop and look more closely, you will discover that you are being attacked with an incredible lie about your Father in heaven.

It is the same lie that Eve succumbed to in the Garden of Eden, believing that God had held something back from her. The serpent told her:

> *You will not surely die. For God knows that in the day you eat of it your eyes will be opened and you will be like God, knowing good and evil.*
>
> (Genesis 3:4-5)

As we saw earlier, Paul tells us that all grace is available to us today and always, and much more, that we would have all sufficiency in all things (2 Corinthians 9:8). Again, not just sufficiency in some things. God wants us to have an all sufficiency in every area of our lives. If you:

> ...honour the Lord with your possessions, and the firstfruits of all your increase; so your barns will be filled with plenty and your vats will overflow with new wine.
>
> (Proverbs 3:9-10)

The word I want you to pay particular attention to is "abundance". The Father's favor for your life is wrapped up in this abundance, for it is the heart of the Father that His sons would have abundance for themselves and their families.

One of the major reasons that the prodigal son's heart turned back to his father was that there was abundance in his father's house even for the servants. The Bible recounts that:

> ...when he came to himself, he said, how many of my father's hired servants have bread enough and to spare, and I perish with hunger!
>
> (Luke 15:17)

Before we deal with the Father's favor or "abundance", and how to live in that place of proper relationship with the Father as His sons, let us take a moment to review the blessings that are already ours in the Father's house. As we have already seen:

- ❖ our integrity will position us financially because we are walking in obedience to God;

- ❖ the tithe will protect us financially because of the open heaven over our lives;

- ❖ the offering will honor us financially because honor begets honor;

- ❖ our responsibility disciplines us financially because we have made ourselves accountable to do what needs to be done in the Father's house.

The aspect we will now address is the seed, which will multiply us financially, or bring us into the abundance that is promised (2 Corinthians 9:8). Paul states that:

> ...now may He who supplies seed to the sower, and bread for food, supply and multiply the seed you have sown and increase the fruits of your righteousness.
>
> (2 Corinthians 9:10)

There are two very important words that you should not miss in this statement, and they are "bread" and "seed". The Father gives everyone the ability to gather provision for their daily needs, and the power to come into a place of abundance for their lives.

First, the Father supplies bread for food, in other words, all that pertains to our needs in life. This thought is reinforced by the prophet Isaiah who said:

> *For as the rain comes down, and the snow from heaven, and do not return there, but water the earth, and make it bring forth and bud, that it may give seed to the sower and bread to the eater.*
> (Isaiah 55:10)

The Word says that the Father gives us bread for food and seed for sowing. No matter what our socioeconomic situation is, this is an indisputable fact. Let these points filter deep into your heart. I believe that if we get hold of them we will enter into a wonderful lifestyle of financial freedom in the Father's house.

Let's look at seed in more detail. There are a number of uses for seed but the major use I want to cover is that it needs to be sown in order for the seed to reach the potential for which it was created. Jesus told us that:

father's financial favour

> ...unless a grain of wheat falls into the ground and dies, it remains alone; but if it dies, it produces much grain.
>
> (John 12:24)

The Father gives us seed to sow, and if we do what He requires of us then we will have a harvest. It is from this harvest that we will enter this wonderful life of abundance. As we saw earlier, God is able:

> ...to make all grace abound toward you, that you, always having all sufficiency in all things, may have an abundance for every good work.
>
> (2 Corinthians 9:8)

Many people seek to be well off financially, that is, they seek to have more than they need for life and living. Few understand that the Father has placed within the hands of all His sons the power to get wealth or abundance (that is, more than we need). We read in the Bible that:

> ...you shall remember the Lord your God, for it is He who gives you power to get wealth, that He may establish His covenant which He swore to your fathers, as it is this day.
>
> (Deuteronomy 8:18)

The power of abundance can be found in the seed and there is always a guarantee that there will be a

the father's favour

harvest if we sow the seed. He who...

> *...sows sparingly will also reap sparingly, and he who sows bountifully will also reap bountifully.*
> (2 Corinthians 9:6)

Galatians, chapter six, also tells us that whatever is sown shall be reaped. The important thing to understand is that we have to actually sow the seed.

There are many reasons why the seed does not get sown, but I would like to focus on four of them:

1. We are fearful about sowing seed.
2. We give away the seed.
3. We eat the seed.
4. The seed has been destroyed because of debt or poor decision making.

Now, let us look at each of these in more detail.

fearful of sowing...

First, we are fearful about sowing the seed because of the circumstances which are confronting us at the time. These circumstances rob us from sowing the seed and therefore obeying the Father who gave us the seed in the first place. While our eyes are filled with the circumstances of life, especially if we perceive them to be negative, then we will not sow.

The writer of Ecclesiastes put it this way, that *"whoever observes the wind will not sow; and whoever regards the clouds will not reap"* (Ecclesiastes 11:4 New Revised Standard Version). If we look for a perfect time to sow the seed, that is, when there is no wind, or the climatic conditions are perfect, or every circumstance is in our favor, there will not be a harvest for our life. We will not know the joy of abundance.

The time to sow is when you need a harvest, and a harvest is required for you to enter into this joy of abundance. The Bible says:

> ...*in the morning sow your seed, and at evening do not let your hands be idle; for you do not know which will prosper, this or that, or whether both alike will be good.*
>
> (Ecclesiastes 11:6 NRSV)

Sowing the seed is an act of faith. While you have the seed in your hand, you retain control of it or, as Jesus said, it abides alone. However, the moment you plant it, you release control and pass it over to the Father, and He has already promised that He gives the power to get wealth.

You can see the release of that power as you relinquish control of the seed, for Father has already determined what life will be in the seed that you have planted.

> *What you sow you do not sow that body that shall be, but mere grain; perhaps wheat or some other grain. But God gives it a body as He pleases, and to each seed its own body.*
> (1 Corinthians 15:37-38)

giving away the seed...

The second reason we can fail to sow seed is that we have given it away. This is one of the major reasons why the sons of the Father's house do not live in the realm of abundance. They have been taught to give or sow the seed away from their area of responsibility. However, we have to sow in order to reap. Jesus told us that the sower went out to sow his seed. The question I would like to pose to the reader is, "Where did he actually sow the seed?" This is a fundamental truth that is not being taught about sowing.

Where does any farmer sow his seed? The obvious answer is "in the ground", but what ground? Well, a farmer always sows the seed in his own farm, and we need to take note of this point, because it is only from his own farm that he will receive a harvest. If he was to give his seed to someone else, then there is no harvest for him. Likewise, if he was to sow his seed in someone else's soil (or farm), then there is no harvest for him. The key to reaping a harvest is to sow the seed that the Father has given to you into your own farm.

Too many Christians have been asked to sow the seed that is provided by the Father into "this ministry" or "this project" or "this mission" or "this minister". The sad fact about this type of teaching (even though the intention may be totally honorable) is that there is no harvest for the farmer who gives away his seed. You cannot sow to a person, or ministry, or minister and expect a harvest. There is only one place that you should sow the seed and that is in your own farm.

Ask yourself this question – are you living a life that has the abundance of the Father flowing through it? Have you sowed many times in obedience to a servant of the Lord whom you've heard in church or on television or some other place, believing that what you sow you shall reap? Have you heard all the promises quoted from the Word that God will do this or that for you, and yet you are not living a life where you are in abundance or in excess?

The Father has given to all of us bread for food and seed for sowing – not for giving away. The seed must be sown in your farm. We will look at how to give a little later in this chapter.

The question that is raised many times with me in the sharing of this truth is "Where is my farm?" I believe your farm is where God places you – in His church. Your farm is not a ministry, but rather a body, because *"God has set the members, each one of them, in the body just as He pleased"* (1 Corinthians 12:18). It is in our own body, or church, where we should extend our faith and sow the seed that has been provided for us. It is there where we let go of control of the seed and let the Father give life to it as He has promised.

The reason some Christians have succumbed to giving away their seed is that they have a great desire to feel a part of a larger ministry, or a particular ministry that is achieving great things for God. There is nothing wrong with these desires, but there is no harvest for them – no matter how good the intention. There is no harvest for them because those ministries are not part of their own farm.

Some people find that it is easier to give away seed to other ministries. It is actually far easier to give your seed away than it is to sow it, because with sowing comes a responsibility to tend the seed and

father's financial favour

watch over it. When you sow seed in your farm, you have a responsibility to fertilize it and to water it with prayer. The reality is that if you give your seed away to another farmer (minister) they can buy a bigger tractor to work their farm (ministry). However, you will not have a harvest. You can fast and pray yourself to a standstill, but it will not bring you a harvest, because only the seed sown in your farm brings the harvest.

Someone once asked me "Isn't the world our farm?" There is a truth to that, but if we can't look after the patch that the Lord has given to us (our own church), we will never be able to look after the harvest of the world. If we follow the patterns God gives us there is a guaranteed harvest, for Father gives body to the seed.

Wanting to be part of a successful ministry is not wrong in itself, but look at your heart and see if your heart is in the farm where Father placed you. Jesus warned us that *"where your treasure is, there your heart will be also"* (Matthew 6:21). The fact is that if your heart is not in your church, your treasure will not be there, and you will not sow the seed there either. Inevitably there will be no harvest. The Father gives us bread for food and seed for sowing because it is the seed that multiplies us financially, giving us abundance.

There is a wonderful example of this principle found in the book of Genesis:

> There was a famine in the land, besides the first famine that was in the days of Abraham. And Isaac went to Abimelech king of the Philistines, in Gerar. Then the Lord appeared to him and said: Do not go down to Egypt; live in the land of which I shall tell you...So Isaac dwelt in Gerar...then Isaac sowed in that land, and reaped in the same year a hundredfold; and the Lord blessed him. The man began to prosper, and continued prospering until he became very prosperous.
>
> (Genesis 26:1-13)

Did you notice where Isaac planted the seed? He planted the seed in the place where God had placed him and nowhere else. Notice also that he was not governed by the circumstances of the time, for the Bible says that there was a famine in the land. Despite the famine, Isaac planted. The result was that he prospered and had abundance over and above what he needed.

eating the seed...

The third reason we can fail to sow seed, is that because of a lack of budgeting skills, we eat the seed instead of sowing it. It certainly doesn't take much to understand that if you eat the seed then you cannot, and will not have a harvest because the seed is not sown. A wise farmer knows that he has to store the seed he has until there comes a time to sow, and that no matter how difficult circumstances become, he can't afford to eat it because he may only get one meal out of it.

If you grind the seed into flour and make a loaf of bread this may even provide a meal for your family, and it may appear that you are good provider, but the reality of the situation is you are only providing one meal and the hunger will return. It is far better to store the seed until there is an opportunity to sow it in your farm. The Father has placed within our grasp the power to get wealth. This power is in the seed – but there must be sowing, not eating.

debt and poor decision making...

Fourth, the seed can be destroyed because of debt and/or poor financial decision-making. We live in an age where many of the transactions of life are made with credit cards, or the "plastic fantastic" as I like to call it! It is sad but true that many sons have switched the control of their lives from the Father to these credit cards. Instead of reaching out, believing, and surrendering to what God is doing in their lives, they reach for an alternate savior in the form of the "plastic fantastic".

I believe that the definition of debt is being in a position of owing to anyone an amount which cannot be repaid without putting oneself into an extreme turmoil that challenges one's righteous stand. The Bible warns us to:

> ...owe no-one anything except to love one another, for he who loves another has fulfilled the law.
> (Romans 13:8)

Debt will destroy the seed that has been given to you to bring abundance to your life, and the problems with debt are many.

Debt can dress you up as one that has affluence, but without the corresponding lack of restraint and improvement that comes with true prosperity. Debt can provide the appearance of security when we are on the threshold of disaster. However, debt strangles or stifles our self-control. It attacks the fruit of the spirit in a son's life, *"for the fruit of the spirit is self control"* (Galatians 5:23) and where there is no self control this will lead to irresponsibility. Debt, when left to its own devices, can take us beyond the parameters of self-control. A lack of self control loosens the restraints that hold us strong and steady.

Debt is a major cause of worry and arguments in many relationships. When God was instructing His people about the financial order that they were to follow, He instructed them not to borrow. He told them:

> ...the Lord will open to you His good treasure, the heavens, to give the rain to your land in its season, and to bless all the work of your hand. You shall lend to many nations, but you shall not borrow.
>
> (Deuteronomy 28:12)

God wants us to trust Him and not the plastic fantastic, because debt causes the heart to lean toward irresponsibility. When we rely on credit, and don't take control of our lives – that is, every time we choose not to pay by cash or cheque ("check" in the U.S.), or direct debit from our account, it lulls us into a false sense of security. When the credit card becomes the savior, the seed that you are supposed to plant to ensure a harvest is instead harvested by the bank or financial institution you are dealing with. Credit cards are not given to you because you are financially capable and can handle your money, they are given to you so that the seed and the life of that seed can be gathered away from you and stored in the silos of the world.

If you cannot pay off your credit card in a reasonable period of time (my suggestion would be in two to three payments after receiving the bill) then you should see this as a sign that your seed is about to leave your house and will never be planted. You should see this as a sign that you are no longer a candidate for abundance. You should take the card and destroy it, because it controls you and you do not control it. Go to your financial institution and ask them how much you will owe them in ten years time if you continue only to pay the minimum amount required each month. The amount may shock you.

If you have to have a "plastic fantastic", then at least make it a charge card. This is the type of card where you have to pay the whole debt in one payment, and there is no interest and therefore no way of getting into serious debt. The fruit of the Spirit is self-control, and you need this self-control to avoid accumulating bad debt.

Proverbs tells us that *"the rich rules over the poor and the borrower is servant to the lender"* (Proverbs 22:7). Debt will lose you friendships, especially if you borrow from friends and don't repay. It will certainly test the depth and reality of the friendship.

The Word tells us that:

God is able to make all grace abound toward you,

that you, always having all sufficiency in all things, may have an abundance for every good work.
(2 Corinthians 9:8)

Debt also hinders the ongoing spreading of the gospel and good works, for there is no seed to sow, no harvest to reap, and no abundance to enjoy or use for others.

The first thing that we need to do when we find ourselves in debt is to take responsibility for it. If we don't take responsibility for it, we will not do anything about the problem and will blame other people or our circumstances for the debt. The road to freedom is to take responsibility.

The next thing we must do is to formulate a plan to decrease or destroy the debt. This involves making a decision not to spend any more on our self than we need to. As an orphan I learned to cut the cloth according to the pattern that I had to live with. In other words I had to live according to what I had, rather than what I did not have.

To deal with debt we need to strike at it very hard. For example, if there is a large debt that needs to be serviced, then I would not take a holiday or upgrade the car or purchase anything out of want rather than need, otherwise the debt will continue to grow. The Bible emphasizes that:

> *...a good name is to be chosen rather than great riches, loving favour rather than silver and gold.*
> (**Proverbs 22:1**)

If your name is of any value to you, then take stock of your life and address this problem.

Now let me highlight this point – the Father gives the seed to all of us, no matter what our socio-economic situation, so that we can sow and reap a harvest. The harvest is guaranteed in the seed, because what we sow we shall also reap, and Father gives body to the seed. We discussed earlier that if we give away the seed, eat it, don't sow it, or allow debt to destroy it, then there will not be a harvest.

Many questions have arisen as I have shared these truths around the world, and the two that are most prevalent are "What happens to the poor?" or "If I don't sow to other Christian ministries (that is outside of my local church) then how do they receive their support?" In answer to the first question, the reality is you never sow to the poor; you always give to the poor. As we saw earlier, this is part of our Christian responsibility because:

> *...he who has pity on the poor lends to the Lord and He will pay back what he has given.*
> (**Proverbs 19:17**)

In answer to the second question, we know that:

> *God is able to make all grace abound toward you, that you, always having all sufficiency in all things, may have an abundance for every good work.*
>
> (2 Corinthians 9:8)

The key here is that you may have "an abundance" for every good work. All these other ministries that are not part of your local church should be supported from the abundance that comes from sowing the seed, and not from the seed itself.

However, none of this is possible if the seed leaves the farm (or church) in any way, shape or form. The Father wants us to be in abundance so that we can then support every good work. He gives us the power and the joy of this, and it is all found in the seed that He supplies to us in the first place.

A lot of teaching over the years has resulted in the seed being taken out of the hands of the church and placed in the hands of other ministries. There has been an emphasis on a doctrine of partnership, and a doctrine of covenant connection, but these have done nothing to bring about a harvest for the giver. All that it has achieved is to remove the seed from the people of God and the church, negate their ability to reap a harvest and leave many good works unsupported.

God's tithe, His offering, and the seed are not meant to support any ministry outside of the local church. All other ministries should be supported by our abundance. One of the main purposes of this book is to demonstrate that our Father has given to us the power to live in abundance. From this abundance we have a responsibility to support good works, and He gives us the power to judge what, and where, these good works are.

Another question that often arises is "How do I know what a seed is?" Remember that Father has given you bread for food and seed for sowing. Bread is the provision the Father provides for your life and family needs. It speaks about life supply. So the simple answer is that "seed" is whatever you have left over after your bread, or your life's supply. This may only be a few dollars. However, it is provided by the Father so that you can begin to live a life of faith, trust and freedom.

We only need to sow one seed to begin a harvest. For example, if you planted one corn (maize) you would at least expect one head of corn as a harvest, and the head would have about two hundred seeds. Already the abundance is beginning to flow! If you

father's financial favour

now plant one hundred of those seeds you would expect at least a harvest of one hundred heads which would translate into twenty thousand seeds, enabling you to have an abundance for every good work.

If you are so far in debt that this seems unattainable to you, let me help you. Your heavenly Father knows and understands your situation and He will often send extra seed along to you so that you can begin to see your way clear. Unfortunately, many of us don't recognize it when it comes along. Often, when a gift does come our way (whether large or small), we look at it from the point of view that it will not meet the need of our debt that is strangling the life out of us.

We fail to realize that it is in fact a seed that Father has sent our way. In this situation, it is best to take some of the gift to pay some of the debt, and then take the rest and sow your way into victory. When you go before Father, thank Him for the seed and sow into your farm, you will see life come your way. You will start a lifestyle that you will never be able to walk away from. Soon you will have an abundance for every good work and the joy of the Lord will again return to your life.

If you adopt these principles for your life, you will know how to walk in the Father's financial favor. The tithe, the offering, the responsibilities, and the seed all belong in the Father's house (the Church). The abundance belongs to you, given so that you can support every good work. This whole concept puts Father back in control of all areas of our life. Now may:

> *He who supplies seed to the sower, and bread for food, supply and multiply the seed you have sown and increase the fruits of your righteousness.*
> (2 Corinthians 9:10)

father's financial favour

Chapter 6

the father's delight

The lifestyle that the Father has for all His sons is one where your integrity positions you financially, the return of God's tithe protects you financially, your offering to God honors you financially, your responsibility disciplines you financially, and your seed multiplies you financially.

When we enter this lifestyle we bring incredible joy to the Father as He watches His sons experience life with His Kingdom as their perspective. No matter how much His sons have or don't have as far as resources are concerned, the determination of their hearts is to put the Kingdom of God first. Every opportunity that comes their way is seen as an opportunity to extend the Kingdom, and their lives are a living investment.

father's financial favour

Over the course of this chapter I would like to take a closer look at this "Kingdom Investment" and how it affects the life of the sons in the Father's house.

a man's gift makes room for him ...

In the Bible we read that *"a man's gift makes room for him, and brings him before great men"* (Proverbs 18:16). I like the emphasis that the New International Version places on this Scripture where "a gift opens the way for the giver and ushers him into the presence of the great". Every time we make an investment into the Kingdom of God – no matter how large or small – we realize a dividend on our investment.

Let's look at an example of this in the second book of Kings. For many years, whenever Elisha the prophet passed by the house of a particular Shunammite family, he would stop and have a meal with them. As time went on, and the woman of the house came to realize that the prophet was totally reliant on the Lord to supply all that he had in life, she was moved to do more than simply make Elisha a meal.

So the Shunammite woman said to her husband:

...please, let us make a small upper room on the

wall; and let us put a bed for him there, and a table and a chair and a lamp stand; so it will be, whenever he comes to us, he can turn in there.

(2 Kings 4:10)

Her husband was in agreement with her, and they decided to invest into the Prophet's life and ministry by building a room on the side of the wall of the house so that he could not only enjoy a meal, but have his own space in which to retire and rest. This Shunammite woman received a return on her investment. The Bible tells us that:

...he who receives a prophet in the name of a prophet shall receive a prophet's reward. And he who receives a righteous man in the name of a righteous man shall receive a righteous man's reward.

(Matthew 10:41)

Elisha asked his servant what could be done for the family, as there was no doubt that he wanted to return kindness for kindness in some way. Gehazi told him that the woman's husband was old and that there was no son in the house. Gehazi pointed out that the woman's purpose in life, that is, bringing forth life, had not yet been realized. So then Elisha asked Gehazi to bring the woman to him. He spoke life into the situation and at the appointed time a son was born.

The woman's investment into the life and ministry of the servant of the Lord was now giving her a return – new life where previously there was no life. Her gift of a meal every time Elisha passed by brought her before great men and her investment in the man of God and his ministry brought life to her womb.

Later in the same chapter (verse twenty one) we see that the child died in the arms of his mother. However, the death of her son did not deter the woman from receiving an ongoing return from the investment she had made. This child was the product of her investment. The prophet spoke life into her and life was produced, and that same word was still living even though the child had died. So she went back to see Elisha. Her husband asked her why she was going to see the prophet, and she replied *"It is well"* (2 Kings 4:26).

This woman had received a return on her investment, and believed that her return (her child) was secure. The ongoing well-being of her child was assured in her heart because the Word had life in it. The woman would not leave the prophet until he came and confirmed the Word spoken into being, and life had come back into the child. She had invested in the Kingdom of God, and she had received a great return for her investment. This same investment assured the ongoing well being of the child, despite the circumstances that life threw her way.

This family is a great example of the need for all of us to build or make more room in our lives to accommodate the Father and His presence, and to extend ourselves to the servants of the Lord if it is within our power to do so. The Shunammite woman made room, and she enjoyed the Kingdom benefits because a gift opens the way for the giver and ushers him into the presence of the great Father.

kingdom investment...

In the Gospel of John, we have the wonderful story of a woman of Samaria who met with Jesus at a well (John 4:7). This confrontation has often been used as an illustration of personal evangelism, and it is a great example of that. However, this same passage of Scripture can also be read from an investment point of view. The first thing that Jesus did when the Samaritan woman came to draw water was to ask her for something, and He said to her "Give Me a drink". Jesus was asking this woman to make an investment in His life.

Now, while a drink of water doesn't sound like much of an investment, a principle was about to be released for her if she responded positively to Jesus' request. As we saw earlier, a gift opens the way for the giver and ushers them into the presence of the great. There was a reward that this woman was about to collect because of her act of kindness to Jesus, because:

> ...whoever gives you a cup of water to drink in My name, because you belong to Christ, assuredly, I say to you, he will by no means lose his reward.
> (Mark 9:41)

We can spiritualize the encounter that Jesus had with the Samaritan woman, or the question that He asked her, but the simple fact is that Jesus was thirsty. He had come to the well looking for a drink but had no container in which to get the water out of the well. There are many instances in our lives where God will send people in need across our path who have a simple need, to see how, or if, we will respond to that need.

The Samaritan woman responded to the need that Jesus had, even though a major cultural barrier existed between them. By drawing a simple drink of water, she was drawing a reward from Jesus, and we read that He shared about the eternal life that she could have.

There is nothing missed by the Father as we

respond to the needs that He sends our way, and the Bible tells us that:

> ...*your charitable deed may be in secret; and your Father who sees in secret will Himself reward you openly.*
> (Matthew 6:4)

As we have seen, the Samaritan woman's investment of a drink of water did not seem like much. However, it illustrates the fact that it is never the size of the investment that's important, but the heart response behind the investment that the Father is looking for.

Jesus saw a poor woman putting an offering to God in the treasury of the temple and He called His disciples to Him and said:

> *Truly I say to you that this poor widow has put in more than all; for all these out of their abundance have put in offerings for God, but she out of her poverty put in all the livelihood that she had.*
> (Luke 21:2-4)

It was not the amount of her offering that He was referring to, even though He said it was her entire livelihood; it was her heart attitude in giving it to God that touched the heart of Jesus.

The Samarian woman's relatively small investment reaped her an eternal dividend. She gave a drink of well water to Jesus and in return, He gave her living water. What a return this was! Let's look at it more closely:

1. He gave her living water for well water. Jesus answered and said to her:

If you knew the gift of God, and who it is who says to you, 'Give Me a drink,' you would have asked Him, and He would have given you living water.

(John 4:10)

2. He gave her restoration because:

...whoever drinks of the water that I shall give him will never thirst. But the water that I shall give him will become in him a fountain of water springing up into everlasting life.

(John 4:14)

3. He gave her a ministry of reconciliation to those that had used her. The Samaritan woman had trouble with relationships with men. When she received the water of life from Jesus, the Scripture says she went back into the city and said to the men:

Come see a Man who told me all things that I ever did. Could this be the Christ?

(John 4:29).

4. He gave her the promise of a fountain of flowing water. The Bible tells us that this was fulfilled when many of the Samaritans of that city believed in Him because of the word of the woman who testified to them that "he told me all that I ever did" (John 4:39).

In one of Rodney Howard Brown's great healing and evangelism crusades I heard him say, "This woman gave to Jesus water from the well and Jesus made her a well for a whole city". He went on to say that unless we become a well for the world we will always have to come back to the well ourselves. The Samaritan woman's gift opened the way for her and ushered her into the presence of the great, and fulfilled the prophecy that Jesus gave to all of us, that is:

> ...the water that I shall give him will become in him a fountain of water springing up into everlasting life.
> (John 4:14)

kingdom provision . . .

There are many examples given in the Bible of where God used people to provide for His servants. One such story involved a widow woman of Zarephath who was in a very desperate situation.

father's financial favour

God used her desperate situation to provide for His prophet Elijah. The word of the Lord came to Elijah, saying:

> *Arise, go to Zarephath, which belongs to Sidon, and dwell there. See, I have commanded a widow there to provide for you.*
>
> (1 Kings 17:8-9)

There are people who God prepares to meet the needs of His servants, and in doing this He prepares them to make an investment into someone else's life. In this particular case, it was a widow woman who was at the end of her life's provision. One of the great challenges of this word is the fact that the Lord told Elijah in advance that a widow would provide for him. It stretches the paradigm of our thinking in terms of how we think our Father will meet our needs and the needs of others.

One of the things I love about this story is that it is so far removed from how we would deal with the situation if it happened to us, or how we would handle this woman and her desperate situation. When we first see her, she was:

> *...gathering a couple of sticks that I may go in and prepare it for myself and my son, that we may eat it, and die.*
>
> (1 Kings 17:12)

When Elijah finds this woman, the first thing he does is to ask her for a cup of water, then a morsel of bread. Whether he was aware of her situation or not, the prophet asked for some of her need to meet his own need and in doing so, he provided an opportunity for her to make an investment into his life. I wonder how many people would be offended if a servant of the Lord did that today?

People who get upset about these circumstances often allow poverty thinking rather than Kingdom thinking to rule their lives. They have great compassion, however because they are not Kingdom oriented, their compassion looks only at the situation of the person and can't see what God is about to do. Their thinking ends up robbing the servant of God from stepping into a miracle of provision, and robs them of the incredible joy of investing into the servant's life. Remember that Jesus said *"It is more blessed to give than to receive"* (Acts 20:35b).

As I was growing in grace and the purposes of the Father for my life in my church, I was faced with a similar situation to the widow of Zarephath. I was not facing circumstances where I was down to my last meal and preparing to die, but I was in a very precarious situation. I had dislocated my knee and could not work. I had no health or medical insurance,

father's financial favour

and so any savings that I had were eaten up with medical bills.

One night my Pastor was addressing the congregation and stated that he believed God was speaking to people in the service about the need to make an investment into the Kingdom of God for their sakes. I felt the touch of the Lord and I began to argue with Him about what I did not have. He reminded me of what I "did" have, which was thirty dollars in my wallet. He also pointed out that this same thirty dollars would not meet the food bill nor would it pay the rent that was due. So I stopped arguing and gave twenty dollars to the Kingdom of God, keeping ten dollars for a hamburger after the service!

That night when I returned home I discovered to my amazement, there was two hundred dollars placed under the door of the apartment that I was living in. I received an instant return on the small investment that was made.

What I did not realize was that God was preparing me to enter into a miracle of provision. All He was waiting for was my heart's response to Him. He was waiting for the Father's desire to take root in my heart. For six months, the Father's financial favor was on my life until I was once more able to provide for myself. So don't let the circumstances that you find yourself in rob you from being a blessing and from making an investment into the Kingdom of God – whether that be toward a servant of the Lord, or in obedience when God speaks to you.

Elijah did not let the circumstances of the woman's life rob her of an opportunity to make an investment into his life even though her investment was only a cup of water and a morsel of bread. Because she responded from a willing heart, she began to realize a dividend on her investment – the dividend that God had reserved for her life and family. God stated that *"the bin of flour shall not be used up, nor shall the jar of oil run dry, until the day the Lord sends rain on the earth"* (1 Kings 17:14). Her small investment was given with the right heart attitude.

God loves a cheerful giver, and she brought delight to her heavenly Father. The return she received was the supernatural provision of flour and oil until the rains came, but it did not stop there, for her investment also brought back the life of her child.

The ongoing relationship that had been started by the Lord, and the response of the woman to the prophet gave her the liberty to approach him and make a greater demand on the investment she had made in his life. Elijah:

father's financial favour

> ...took the child and brought him down from the upper room into the house, and gave him to his mother. And Elijah said, "See, your son lives!
>
> (1 Kings 17:23)

A gift opens the way for the giver and ushers him into the presence of the great.

kingdom blessing...

There's a wonderful story in Luke chapter five, which is full of this truth of investment. Jesus needed a boat to preach from so he asked Simon Peter for the loan of his boat.

> He got into one of the boats, which was Simon's, and asked him to put out a little from the land, and He sat down and taught the multitudes from the boat.
>
> (Luke 5:3)

Jesus was asking Peter to provide what he had for Him to enable Him to preach the Word. He was asking Peter to make an investment into His ministry of preaching the gospel. There will be times in our lives where our Father will bring opportunities across our paths to help with spreading on the gospel, just like this practical example of the use of Peter's boat.

the father's delight

The interesting thing about this passage is that as you read it, you discover that Peter had toiled all night and had caught nothing. It was at this vulnerable point that Jesus asked him for the use of his boat. As gifted as Peter was as a fisherman, and as good as the vessel was for fishing, on this particular night both Peter and the boat did not reach their potential. Yet, when the boat was placed into the hands of the Lord for the sake of the gospel, the potential of the vessel began to change.

When Jesus had finished with the boat, He gave it back to Peter, and said to him *"Launch out into the deep and let down your nets for a catch"* (Luke 5:4). There are times in most of our lives when we invest in things that don't seem to work out the way that we wanted them to. However, when we place these same things in the hand of Jesus then we start to see a different result.

As Peter gave over the use of his boat for the gospel as an investment, his provision of fish (that is, the return on his investment) was already gathering. As Rodney Howard Brown has said "They were just waiting for a reason to gather". Peter's investment – the use of something which had produced nothing that night – brought him a great return.

Peter had a net-breaking experience. When Peter

dropped the net over the other side of the boat, *"they caught a great number of fish, and their net was breaking"* (Luke 5:6). But the return did not terminate with this net-breaking experience. This great supernatural provision also provided Peter with a spiritual awaking. When Simon Peter saw it, he fell down at Jesus' knees saying, *"Depart from me, for I am a sinful man, O Lord!"* (Luke 5:8). Peter's business was catching fish and Jesus promised he would become a fisher of men, telling him *"Do not be afraid. From now on you will catch men"* (Luke 5:10).

Peter's response to Jesus that day in his willingness to allow Him the use of his boat and his obedience to the Word, not only brought a great return to him and his family, but also affected his partners and their families. There were so many fish that they:

> ...signaled to their partners in the other boat to come and help them, and they came and filled both the boats, so that they began to sink.
>
> (Luke 5:7)

Your investment in the Kingdom of God will always bring about an ongoing overflow to those around you.

kingdom return . . .

In John's gospel we read a very familiar story of the feeding of the five thousand with five loaves and two fish (chapter six). There are so many wonderful truths in this passage, and one of the truths I would like to explore is what resulted from a little boy surrendering his lunch to Jesus.

A multitude of people followed Jesus out into the wilderness and there was nothing to feed them with. Andrew, who was the brother of Peter, came up with the seemingly feeble solution of a lad with five loaves and two fish to feed a whole crowd. As we saw earlier, it is not the size of the investment that is the issue. It is the response of the heart that is important to God. No matter how little you have in your hand, or how big the solution is that you need, if you place it in the hand of Jesus it will produce outstanding results.

The boy's investment was five loaves and two fish, but the return on that investment affected multitudes. With the fish and bread at his disposal, Jesus blessed it and asked the disciples to start passing it out amongst the crowd of five thousand.

First, we see that a multitude of around five

father's financial favour

thousand people were fed (Mark 6:44). Second, we see that the disciples walked in a level of faith that they had not experienced before. Each time they returned to the basket there was more food, and their faith began to grow as they walked in this miraculous provision. Third, we see the return for the lad who provided the investment of five loaves and two fish, in the twelve baskets of food that were left over.

I wonder who had the job of carrying the twelve baskets that were left over home for the boy. Not that the Bible says so, but it makes sense to me that it would have been the twelve disciples. I have heard a preacher once say that maybe this was their commitment to the lad in thanks for his generous gift.

kingdom cost...

Jesus was visiting at Simon the leper's house. A woman (most likely Mary):

> ...came having an alabaster flask of very costly oil of spikenard. Then she broke the flask and poured it on His head.
>
> (Mark 14:3)

This woman was so taken with Jesus, that at

great cost to herself, she blessed Jesus, who said that she had anointed His body for burial. I love what Jesus says, *"Let her alone. Why do you trouble her? She has done a good work for me"* (Mark 14:6).

Jesus stated that the investment she made was a good work to Him, and He made this statement in response to some of the negative comments that the disciples made as they watched her extravagant outpouring of love. There were some who were "indignant" among themselves and said, *"Why was this fragrant oil wasted?"* (Mark 14:4).

It is amazing how extravagant worship, giving or investment will always cause others to react — especially if they are not as exuberant with their investment or love. What right did the disciples have to comment on her act of love, given that they were not the ones doing it for Jesus?

This precious woman made an investment in the burial of the Lord. Jesus told them that she had anointed His body for burial. Jesus acknowledged her investment and explained the dividend that was realized when He said:

Assuredly, I say to you, wherever this gospel is preached in the whole world, what this woman has done will also be told as a memorial to her.
(Mark 14:9)

father's financial favour

Another wonderful aspect of this that I have heard Rodney Howard Brown mention is that "Only the giver and the receiver were touched by the aroma of such a precious gift. Everyone else smelt it but was not touched by it". Again, Mary's investment into Jesus became a memorial to her, because a gift opens the way for the giver and ushers him into the presence of the great (Proverbs 18:16 NIV).

kingdom vision ...

Finally, I would like to look at a small part of the life of Jesus who, from the age of twelve until the age of thirty, invested into the life, vision and honor of His earthly parents, Joseph and Mary. This was not a small thing, because for eighteen years He carried around with Him the knowledge that He must be about His Father's business, and yet He stayed in obedience to His earthly parents. When He was twelve years old:

> *They went up to Jerusalem according to the custom of the feast. And He said to them, why did you seek Me? Did you not know that I must be about My Father's business?*
>
> (Luke 2:42-49)

the father's delight

The Bible says that though He was a Son, He learned obedience by the things He suffered (Heb. 5:8). We all know about the suffering He experienced on the cross, but what about the eighteen years of suffering He experienced when He was walking in obedience, all the while knowing that there was a greater call on His life? When He was investing into the vision of His earthly father, yet burdened with the call of His heavenly Father?

We can also make this investment. When we serve our earthly father's vision and honor him, there is a return that comes to us also. If you "honour your father and mother, which is the first commandment with promise *"it may be well with you and you may live long on the earth"* (Ephesians 6:2-3).

Jesus invested into His earthly parents and the return He received was to *"increase in wisdom and stature and in favor with God and men"* (Luke 2:52). The Bible tells us He learned obedience through what He suffered. Eighteen years of waiting to be realized in the ministry was His investment. He then invested his life for all so that none would perish. The return is that in eternity there will be myriads of people from all races, nations and tongues that will declare He is worthy.

father's financial favour

Even the traitor's thirty pieces of silver which were used to buy the potter's field (Matthew 27) was used to bring a return. In Jesus' death by the hand of a traitor, the price of His betrayal brought all the broken pieces of clay from the useless vessels that were thrown over the wall of the city into the potter's field. How many of us have felt at some time in our lives that we are nothing but useless clay vessels that are broken, used and abused? In the hand of the Lord nothing is useless.

The Father invested Jesus for your life. As a son of the Father will you now do that which will bring a return for His Kingdom? Investing is a Godly thing which will always bring a return. Sometimes investment is asked for, sometimes it is given out of a generous heart, and other times it is prompted by the Lord to motivate a heart response. I hope that the principles that have been shared in this book will inspire you and cause you to enter into the Father's financial favor for your life.

conclusion . . .

In the Father's house all His sons are equal, and all share in His inheritance. However, we all have to realize that we must grow up and mature as sons so that we are not tempted to just stay as children −

especially in the area of the Father's finances.

We need to grow, just as Jesus *"increased in wisdom and stature, and in favour with God and men"* (Luke 2:52). If we do not grow up, there is a real danger that we will never enter into the favor that the Father wants to give us in this realm. In Galatians we read that:

> *...the heir, as long as he is a child, does not differ at all from a slave, though he is master of all, we may be master of all and heirs to all.*
> (Galatians 4:1)

If we remain as a child the Bible says that we are no different from a slave. Everything is available to us, but we don't get to enjoy it. That is why I implore you to take hold of the truth of the Word of God especially on the subject of finances, and be a blessing to the Kingdom of God, rather than always looking for a blessing.

During my life as a Christian, and as a preacher, I have heard many people speak about how to use the Word of God to help our Christian growth. However, I doubt I've ever heard anything more impacting than a comment made by a British preacher by the name of Clive Pick. He said if you want to get the devil off your finances, then attack him with the Word financially – literally!

father's financial favour

Clive used the Scripture found in James which states *"therefore submit to God. Resist the devil and he will flee from you"* (James 4:7). To add emphasis and illustrate his principle, Clive said that when you know you are being attacked in the area of finances, then *"submit to God **financially,** resist the devil **financially,** and he will flee from you **financially**"* (the words in italics are added).

In conclusion, let me re-state the principles that will help us to grow in grace and in the Father's financial favor:

- ❖ In the Father's house our integrity positions us financially because we have responded to the Father in obedience with respect to His finances in His house;

- ❖ The return of God's tithe protects us financially because the windows of heaven are opened over our lives;

- ❖ Our offering to God honors us financially, for honor begets honor;

- ❖ Our responsibility disciplines us financially because we have made ourselves accountable to do what needs to be done in the Father's house where He plants us;

- ❖ The seed that we plant will be multiplied back to us financially because God gives the seed its body.

- ❖ The investments we make for the Kingdom of God empower us financially because there is now a freedom in our lives that is not dependent on what we have or may not have.

My hope and prayer is that this book has helped you and will continue to help you walk in the financial freedom that is yours in the Father's House.

I will finish as I started, with the central truth that ...

> *God so loved the world that He gave His only begotten Son, that whoever believes in Him should not perish but have everlasting life.*
> (John 3:16)

That is the true basis of the *father's financial favour* for you.

father's financial favour

references

Jastrow Jr. M., *Burnt Offering*. (Biblical data) JewishEncyclopedia.com

Fowler, H.W. & Fowler, F.G., *The Concise Oxford Dictionary* (1964). Oxford University Press.

Strong, J. *The New Strong's Exhaustive Concordance of the Bible*. (1996) Thomas Nelson.

father's financial favour